Thanks to Calvary:

A Salvific Treatise on the Cross

Kayumba David

Thanks to Calvary: A Salvific Treatise on the Cross

Kayumba David

Published by Kayumba David, 2024.

THANKS TO CALVARY: A SALVIFIC TREATISE ON THE CROSS

First edition. November 7, 2024.

ISBN: 979-8227447807

Written by Kayumba David.

Also by Kayumba David

1
Grow a Backbone and Walk out of an Abusive Marriage

Standalone
Grow a Backbone and Walk out of an Abusive Marriage
HARVESTING ILLUSIONS:The Global Greed and the
Pan-African Paradox
Hope and Healing: A Chaplain's Handbook
HOW TO FAIL A CONTINENT: THE WESTERN GUIDE TO
SUPPORTING DICTATORS AND LOOTING RESOURCES
IN AFRICA
REVERSING TYPE 2 DIABETES NATURALLY
Visas: The Irony of Freedom
A MEETING WITH MAJESTY: THE KING'S CALL TO
HUMANITY
A MEETING WITH MAJESTY: THE KING'S CALL TO
HUMANITY
Visas: The Irony of Freedom
Love Beyond Time A Comedy of Divine Connection
Silent Complicity: State Sovereignty, Global Inaction, and the
Rwandan Genocide
Bridging the Rift: A Pacifist Vision for the Israel-Palestine Future

Thanks to Calvary: A Salvific Treatise on the Cross
The centuries old swindlers

Watch for more at www.zcews.org.

Dedication

To the One who made Calvary a reality—To Jesus Christ, whose cross conquered death, defeated sin, and provided the assurance of eternal salvation.

To my beloved family, who walked this journey of faith with me, and to all who seek the certainty and transformative power of the cross.

May this work glorify Christ and draw you nearer to Him.

Dedication

To the One who made Calvary a reality—

To Jesus Christ, whose cross conquered death, defeated sin, and provided the assurance of eternal salvation.

To my beloved family, who walked this journey of faith with me, and to all who seek the certainty and transformative power of the cross.

May this work glorify Christ and draw you nearer to Him.

Preface

The cross of Jesus Christ is the axis of human history, the event upon which the fate of all creation hinges. This book, *"Thanks to Calvary: A Salvific Treatise on the Cross"*, represents years of contemplation, prayer, and engagement with the profound truths revealed in Scripture. As I delved into the Pauline understanding of the cross, I realized that it offers more than just theological insight; it provides the assurance of salvation, the end of religious striving, and the dawn of grace.

Growing up, I often grappled with questions about salvation, guilt, and whether I was truly "right" with God. It was the teaching of the Apostle Paul, especially his exposition of the cross, that opened my eyes to the finality of Christ's work. I discovered that Calvary was not merely an event to be remembered; it was a reality to be experienced. The cross, as Dr. Desmond Ford once said, is "God's final word on sin and grace" (Ford, *The Cross and Grace*, p. 3). In it, I found hope, freedom, and certainty.

Throughout this work, I draw from esteemed scholars and theologians, including Dr. Ford, Charles Spurgeon, and Hauwar Stanely. These men have illuminated the depths of Pauline theology and the centrality of the cross in ways that continue to inspire and convict me. Their writings have enriched my understanding and compelled me to share these truths with a wider audience.

This book aims to articulate the all-encompassing significance of the cross of Jesus Christ. It is my prayer that as you journey through these pages, you will see the cross not merely as a religious symbol, but as the transformative event that forever changed the cosmos, conquered sin, and offers the assurance of salvation for all who believe. In a world where religious uncertainty often clouds faith, may the message of Calvary shine brightly as a beacon of hope.

Thank you for joining me on this journey. To God alone be the glory.

THANKS TO CALVARY: A SALVIFIC TREATISE ON THE CROSS

Kayumba David

Contents

Introduction

The Centrality of the Cross

The cross of Christ stands as the pinnacle of God's redemptive work and the finality of all religion. It is both the culmination of the Old Testament sacrificial system and the climax of God's redemptive plan for humanity. Without the cross, Christianity becomes devoid of meaning, much like a sky without its sun—empty, dark, and devoid of life. It is the cross that gives depth, light, and clarity to the Christian faith. As Dr. Desmond Ford emphasized, "The cross is the meeting place of divine justice and mercy. It is where sin was condemned and grace triumphed" (Ford, *The Cross of Christ*, p. 45). Through the cross, God revealed the fullness of His love and justice, bringing together two attributes that otherwise seem irreconcilable. Justice demanded the punishment of sin; love offered a pathway to reconciliation.

The uniqueness of the cross lies in its scope and depth. On the one hand, it is a historic event that took place at a specific point in time—a Roman execution that led to the crucifixion of a man named Jesus of Nazareth. On the other hand, it is an eternal and cosmic event whose implications ripple throughout time and space. The cross is not merely a tragedy of human injustice; it is the triumph of divine justice and mercy, achieving cosmic reconciliation between God and creation.

The Intersection of Divine Justice and Mercy

The tension between divine justice and mercy is one that humanity has wrestled with throughout history. How can a holy God, who cannot tolerate sin, also be a merciful God, willing to forgive and restore? The answer is found in the cross. At Calvary, God's justice was fully satisfied because the penalty of sin was paid in full by Jesus Christ, the spotless Lamb. At the same time, God's mercy was fully displayed as He provided salvation for all who believe. In Paul's words, "God made him who had no sin to be sin for us, so that in him we might become the righteousness of God" (2 Corinthians 5:21). Through substitutionary atonement, Christ took upon Himself the punishment we deserved, allowing us to receive His righteousness in exchange.

As Charles Spurgeon once preached, "The justice of God was satisfied by the great sacrifice of Calvary, and the mercy of God was magnified in the pardoning of sinners" (Spurgeon, *Sermons on the Cross*, p. 123). The cross resolves the apparent paradox of God's nature, demonstrating that He is both just and the justifier of those who have faith in Jesus (Romans 3:26).

The Cross: The Anchor of Assurance and the End of Religious Striving

Humanity has long been plagued by religious uncertainty and the striving to earn God's favor through works and rituals. The cross puts an end to all such striving. It declares unequivocally that salvation is not the result of human effort, but the gift of God through faith in Jesus Christ (Ephesians 2:8-9). Dr. Desmond Ford wrote, "Calvary is God's final word on sin, grace, and redemption. It is the assurance that nothing can separate believers from the love of God" (Ford, *The Finality of the Cross*, p. 87). The cross, therefore, serves as the believer's anchor of assurance, silencing doubts and providing certainty of salvation.

Paul, who once boasted in his adherence to the law, came to understand that his righteousness could only be found in Christ and His work on the cross. He wrote to the Galatians, "May I never boast except in the cross of our Lord Jesus Christ, through which the world has been crucified to me, and I to the world" (Galatians 6:14). This radical reorientation from self-righteousness to Christ-centered faith underscores the cross's centrality in Pauline theology.

The Cosmic Scope of the Cross

The cross's significance is not limited to individual salvation. It has cosmic implications that stretch far beyond personal redemption. In Colossians 1:20, Paul proclaims that through the blood of Christ's cross, God reconciled all things, whether on earth or in heaven. The death and resurrection of Jesus ushered in the beginning of a new creation—a creation liberated from the curse of sin and death. Hauwar Stanely writes, "The cross signals not only the redemption of humanity but the renewal of all creation, pointing to the day when every knee will bow and every tongue will confess that Jesus Christ is Lord" (Stanely, *Cosmic Redemption*, p. 110).

The cross, therefore, restores the broken relationship between God and humanity, as well as the entire created order. It is the means by which God is bringing all things into alignment with His will and purpose.

The Personal Transformation of the Cross

While the cross has cosmic implications, its transformative power is deeply personal. It reaches into the human heart, bringing about a change that no self-help effort or religious ritual could ever achieve. Through the cross, believers are not only forgiven; they are also made new creations (2 Corinthians 5:17). The Apostle Paul's own life is a testament to this transformative power. Once a zealous persecutor of Christians, Paul became one of the greatest apostles and missionaries of the Christian faith. He attributed this radical change solely to the grace of God revealed at the cross.

Paul encapsulated this truth when he declared, "I have been crucified with Christ, and I no longer live, but Christ lives in me. The life I now live in the body, I live by faith in the Son of God, who loved me and gave Himself for me" (Galatians 2:20). The cross brings about the death of the old self and the birth of a new life in Christ—a life marked by love, sacrifice, and the fruit of the Spirit.

The Cross: The Fulfillment of God's Promises

The cross also stands as the fulfillment of all of God's promises. From the very beginning, God promised a Redeemer who would crush the serpent's head and restore humanity to Himself (Genesis 3:15). Throughout the Old Testament, prophets foretold the coming of the Messiah who would suffer and die for the sins of the world. All of these promises found their "Yes" in Christ (2 Corinthians 1:20). Through the cross, God demonstrated His faithfulness to His covenant and His commitment to redeem His people.

This salvific treatise seeks to explore the theological, cosmic, and personal dimensions of the cross as revealed in Pauline theology. It is our anchor of assurance, the fulfillment of God's promises, and the end of religious uncertainty. As the Apostle Paul articulated so powerfully, "For I resolved to know nothing while I was with you except Jesus Christ and Him crucified" (1 Corinthians 2:2). From this foundational truth, we will examine how the cross achieves cosmic reconciliation, personal transformation, and the assurance of salvation. In this light, the cross of Christ stands as the pivotal and final word on God's plan for redemption and the source of all hope for a fallen world.

Part 1: The Cosmic Reconciliation

Chapter 1

Heaven and Earth United

The cross of Jesus Christ is far more than a mere event in human history; it is the fulcrum upon which the reconciliation of heaven and earth pivots. The Apostle Paul makes this abundantly clear in Colossians 1:20, where he writes, "Through Him to reconcile all things, whether things on earth or things in heaven, by making peace through His blood, shed on the cross." This statement underscores the cosmic significance of Christ's sacrificial death, presenting it as the divine act that bridges the rift between the Creator and His creation. The cross stands as both the declaration and the instrument of peace, bringing unity to the fragmented realms of existence.

Cosmic Reconciliation: Bridging the Divide

From the moment sin entered the world through Adam, the relationship between heaven and earth was fractured. Humanity's rebellion did not merely disrupt individual relationships with God; it tainted all of creation, leaving it subjected to decay and corruption (Romans 8:20-21). This cosmic disorder is evident in the brokenness and suffering we witness around us—nature groaning under the weight of sin, spiritual powers in rebellion, and humanity estranged from God. The cross addresses and heals this rift by reconciling "all things" to God.

Dr. N.T. Wright explains that "Paul's vision of cosmic reconciliation is rooted in the triumph of Christ on the cross, which defeated the powers that hold creation in bondage" (*Paul and the Faithfulness of God*, p. 345). Wright emphasizes that this reconciliation is not merely symbolic; it is a tangible victory over every power that stands in opposition to God's rule. In Christ's crucifixion, sin, death, and the principalities and powers of darkness were dealt a decisive blow, bringing liberation to a creation held captive.

Key Insight: The Cross as the Vehicle of Cosmic Restoration

The cross is often perceived solely in terms of personal salvation, and while it is deeply personal, its reach extends to the entire cosmos. It is the vehicle through which God is restoring cosmic order, making peace where there was once division. The reconciliation Paul speaks of encompasses both "things on earth and things in heaven," suggesting that no corner of creation is untouched by Christ's redemptive work. Through the cross, God is bringing everything into alignment with His sovereign purpose.

This cosmic dimension underscores the profound truth that Christ's work was not an isolated act for the benefit of a few, but a redemptive initiative that encompasses the entirety of creation. It invites believers to see the world, and their role within it, through the lens of Christ's lordship and restorative mission. Dr. Desmond Ford aptly states, "The cross is the grand centerpiece of cosmic order and renewal. It touches all things visible and invisible, reconciling them back to God's original purpose" (*The Final Word of the Cross*, p. 43).

The Triumph Over Spiritual Powers

Pauline theology consistently emphasizes that Christ's work on the cross was a triumph over spiritual forces that sought to dominate and oppress creation. In Colossians 2:15, Paul writes, "Having disarmed the powers and authorities, He made a public spectacle of them, triumphing over them by the cross." This imagery of triumph, drawn from Roman military victory processions, paints a vivid picture of

Christ leading a procession of vanquished spiritual powers, exposing their defeat to all.

Charles Spurgeon eloquently reflected on this victory, declaring, "The cross is the place where every rebellious power was broken and stripped of its claim. In that moment, the kingdom of darkness was put to shame before all of heaven and earth" (*Sermons on the Victory of the Cross*, p. 221). Dr. Desmond Ford further elaborates, "The cross was a public triumph over all spiritual forces. It exposed the principalities and powers and made a public spectacle of them, bringing the kingdom of darkness to a decisive end" (*The Final Word of the Cross*, p. 67).

The Cross Ends All Human Sacrifices and Vain Efforts to Appease God

For centuries, humanity's attempts to appease the divine often led to rituals, sacrifices, and practices designed to earn favor or avert divine wrath. From ancient pagan sacrifices to the most stringent legalistic observances, human efforts to reach God have been marked by striving, fear, and inadequacy. The cross of Christ brings an end to all such efforts. It declares, once and for all, that no human sacrifice or work can achieve reconciliation with God. Hebrews 10:12-14 asserts, "But when this priest had offered for all time one sacrifice for sins, He sat down at the right hand of God... For by one sacrifice He has made perfect forever those who are being made holy."

Spurgeon captures the essence of this transformative truth: "The death of Christ is the death of all other sacrifices. No more shall bulls and goats bleed to make atonement. Christ's blood has spoken, and it speaks better things" (*The Finished Work of Christ*, p. 75). This finality brings freedom from futile efforts and opens the door to true worship and grace.

Hauwar Stanely echoes this sentiment, stating, "The cross marks the end of humanity's vain attempts to appease a holy God. It declares that salvation is achieved, not by human effort, but by the sovereign work of God in Christ" (*Redemptive Work of Christ*, p. 91).

The Restoration of Creation's Purpose

The reconciliation achieved through the cross goes beyond merely defeating spiritual powers; it restores creation to its intended purpose. In Romans 8:19-21, Paul describes creation as eagerly awaiting the "revelation of the children of God," longing to be liberated from its "bondage to decay." The cross sets in motion this liberation, placing creation on a trajectory toward renewal and restoration. As Hauwar Stanely states, "The cross is God's cosmic reclamation project, reestablishing His reign over a creation that had been marred by sin" (*The Cosmic Cross*, p. 101).

Believers, as the redeemed children of God, play a vital role in this ongoing restoration. Through their lives, the power of the cross continues to be manifested as they live out the victory of Christ, bringing God's kingdom to bear on every aspect of creation—social structures, relationships, communities, and even the natural world. This reality challenges Christians to view their faith not only as a matter of personal piety but as a call to participate in God's grand design of cosmic restoration.

The Cross as a Bridge Between Heaven and Earth

At the heart of this cosmic reconciliation is the cross's role as a bridge between heaven and earth. The imagery of a bridge evokes the idea of access, connection, and restoration of what was previously separated. Christ, through His atoning death, reopens the way for humanity to enter into fellowship with God. Hebrews 10:19-20 states, "Therefore, brothers and sisters, since we have confidence to enter the Most Holy

Place by the blood of Jesus, by a new and living way opened for us through the curtain, that is, His body."

This "new and living way" speaks of unrestricted access to God—a privilege once reserved only for the high priest under the Old Covenant. Now, through the cross, heaven and earth are united, and believers are invited to enter into God's presence with boldness and assurance. As Dr. Ford notes, "The cross is the opening of heaven's gates to all who come by faith. It tears down the walls of separation and brings humanity face to face with God" (*The Cross and Redemption*, p. 102).

Practical Implications for Believers

The cosmic reconciliation achieved through the cross has profound implications for every believer. First, it calls Christians to live as agents of reconciliation, reflecting the peace and unity established by Christ. Paul writes in 2 Corinthians 5:18-19, "All this is from God, who reconciled us to Himself through Christ and gave us the ministry of reconciliation." The cross compels believers to be peacemakers, bridge-builders, and ambassadors of Christ's kingdom in a world still marred by division and strife.

Second, the cosmic dimension of the cross reminds believers that their salvation is part of a grander narrative. They are not isolated recipients of grace; they are participants in God's redemptive mission that spans heaven and earth. This understanding should inspire humility, awe, and a renewed sense of purpose.

The Centrality of Christ's Lordship

Finally, the cosmic reconciliation achieved through the cross underscores the lordship of Christ over all creation. Paul's declaration that "every knee should bow, in heaven and on earth and under the earth, and every tongue acknowledge that Jesus Christ is Lord" (Philippians 2:10-11) is rooted in the victory of the cross. Jesus is not merely a savior of souls; He is the cosmic King who reigns supreme over every aspect of creation.

Conclusion

The cross of Christ unites heaven and earth, reconciling all things to God and bringing peace where there was once enmity. It brings an end to all human sacrifices and vain efforts to appease God, declaring that Christ's sacrifice is sufficient. Through His sacrificial death, Christ defeated the powers of darkness, restored creation's purpose, and provided a bridge for humanity to enter into God's presence. The cosmic scope of this reconciliation invites believers to see their faith in light of God's grand redemptive plan, inspiring them to live as agents of peace, ambassadors of reconciliation, and participants in the ongoing restoration of all things under the lordship of Christ.

Chapter 2

The Defeat of Sin and the Fulfillment of the Law

In his letter to the Romans, the Apostle Paul offers profound insight into the defeat of sin and the fulfillment of the law. He writes, "For what the law was powerless to do because it was weakened by the flesh, God did by sending His own Son in the likeness of sinful flesh to be a sin offering. And so He condemned sin in the flesh, in order that the righteous requirement of the law might be fully met in us, who do not live according to the flesh but according to the Spirit" (Romans 8:3-4). This passage encapsulates the gospel's core message: the law, while good and holy, was incapable of bringing salvation due to humanity's inherent weakness. The cross of Christ achieved what human effort and adherence to the law could not—complete and final justification.

The Inability of the Law and the Triumph of the Cross

Pauline theology emphasizes that the Mosaic Law was given to reveal sin and guide humanity toward righteousness, but it could never provide the power to overcome sin. "For by works of the law no human being will be justified in His sight, since through the law comes knowledge of sin" (Romans 3:20). The law exposed human inability, highlighting our desperate need for a Savior. Dr. Desmond Ford explains, "The law was like a mirror that revealed our sin-stained condition, but it had no power to cleanse us. Only the blood of Christ could wash away our guilt and satisfy the demands of divine justice" (*The Finality of the Cross*, p. 56).

In sending His Son, God accomplished what the law could never achieve. Jesus Christ, the sinless One, took on human flesh, lived in perfect obedience to the law, and willingly became the ultimate sacrifice for sin. His atoning death fulfilled every requirement of the law, satisfying both its demands for justice and its promise of mercy. As Paul writes in Galatians 3:13, "Christ redeemed us from the curse of the law by becoming a curse for us."

Charles Spurgeon, reflecting on the efficacy of Christ's sacrifice, stated, "The death of Christ was the end of all human striving. By His stripes, we are justified, cleansed, and made right before God" (*The Justifying Cross*, p. 129). Spurgeon's words capture the essence of the gospel: Christ's death put an end to the futile efforts of humanity to earn righteousness through works. His finished work on the cross is sufficient for salvation, making every believer righteous before God.

Legal and Relational Aspects of the Cross

The cross of Christ not only fulfilled the legal demands of the law but also addressed the relational breach caused by sin. Legally, sin incurred a penalty—death—that had to be paid. Jesus, as our substitute, bore the full weight of this penalty on the cross. Paul affirms this in 2 Corinthians 5:21, saying, "God made Him who had no sin to be sin for us, so that in Him we might become the righteousness of God." In Christ's death, the penalty for sin was fully paid, satisfying God's justice and liberating us from condemnation.

Simultaneously, the cross healed the relational rift between God and humanity. Sin not only brings guilt but also estrangement from God. The relational aspect of the cross is beautifully illustrated in Paul's words in Ephesians 2:13, "But now in Christ Jesus you who once were far away have been brought near by the blood of Christ." Through His sacrifice, Christ restored the broken relationship between God and humanity, reconciling us to the Father and granting us access to His presence.

Dr. Desmond Ford emphasizes the dual nature of Christ's work on the cross: "Sin had two effects: guilt and estrangement. The cross cured both, meeting the legal requirements and opening the way for intimacy with God" (*The Great Exchange*, p. 92). Ford's insight highlights the completeness of Christ's redemptive work. The cross not only justified us legally but also restored us relationally, bringing us into a loving and personal relationship with God.

The Fulfillment of the Law in Christ's Perfect Obedience

Christ's life of perfect obedience is a crucial aspect of His redemptive work. He did not merely die for our sins; He lived a life of flawless righteousness on our behalf. This active obedience is what qualifies Him as the perfect sacrifice and what enables believers to be clothed in His righteousness. Paul writes in Romans 5:19, "For just as through the disobedience of the one man the many were made sinners, so also through the obedience of the one man the many will be made righteous." Christ's obedience fulfilled every aspect of the law, making Him the only acceptable sacrifice for sin.

Charles Spurgeon captured this profound truth when he wrote, "Our Lord Jesus was not only spotless in His death but also in His life. He fulfilled every jot and tittle of the law so that His righteousness might be imputed to us. In Him, we stand perfect and complete before a holy God" (*Christ's Perfect Obedience*, p. 67).

The Cross as the End of Human Striving

For generations, humanity has attempted to earn God's favor through works, sacrifices, and adherence to religious rules. These efforts, while often sincere, ultimately fall short of achieving true righteousness. The cross of Christ brings an end to this striving. Paul writes in Galatians 2:16, "Know that a person is not justified by the works of the law, but by faith in Jesus Christ. So we, too, have put our faith in Christ Jesus that we may be justified by faith in Christ and not by the works of the law, because by the works of the law no one will be justified."

Dr. Ford states, "Calvary marks the end of human efforts to gain righteousness. It is a declaration that salvation is by grace through faith, and no amount of human striving can add to the completed work of Christ" (*The Cross and Grace*, p. 88). This truth liberates believers from the burden of performance-based religion and invites them into a relationship of grace and faith.

The Cross and the Defeat of Sin's Power

Not only did the cross satisfy the legal demands of the law, but it also broke the power of sin over believers. Paul writes in Romans 6:6-7, "For we know that our old self was crucified with Him so that the body ruled by sin might be done away with, that we should no longer be slaves to sin—because anyone who has died has been set free from sin." Through the cross, believers are no longer under sin's dominion; they are free to live in righteousness.

Hauwar Stanely explains, "The cross not only justifies but sanctifies. It breaks the chains of sin and empowers believers to live holy lives by the Spirit" (*The Cross and Holiness*, p. 142). This dual aspect of the cross—justification and sanctification—demonstrates its all-encompassing power to transform lives.

Conclusion

The cross of Christ achieved what the law and human effort could never accomplish. It fulfilled the law's righteous demands, satisfied divine justice, and defeated the power of sin. As believers, we stand justified and reconciled, not by our works but by Christ's finished work on the cross. Charles Spurgeon summarized this beautifully: "By His stripes, we are justified, cleansed, and made right before God. The cross is the end of all striving and the beginning of true freedom" (*The Justifying Cross*, p. 129). Through His death and resurrection, Christ offers us a new life marked by grace, freedom, and intimate fellowship with God.

Chapter 3

Redemption for Creation

In Romans 8:19-21, Paul writes of creation's deep yearning for liberation: "The creation waits in eager expectation for the children of God to be revealed… in hope that the creation itself will be liberated from its bondage to decay and brought into the freedom and glory of the children of God." This passage underscores a truth often overlooked—the scope of the cross extends beyond individual human redemption. It touches every part of creation, promising liberation, renewal, and transformation. The cross of Christ is the means by which God restores not only fallen humanity but also the entire cosmos. Paul's words portray creation as waiting on tiptoe, straining to see the fulfillment of God's redemptive plan.

The Cosmic Reach of the Cross

The redemption achieved by Christ's sacrifice encompasses every aspect of the created order. It is not limited to the salvation of souls; it is about the renewal of all things. Hauwar Stanely writes, "The cross reverberates through all aspects of the created order, breaking the curse and promising a renewed creation. It is the heartbeat of cosmic restoration" (*The Cosmic Cross*, p. 101). The work of Christ on the cross shatters the curse of sin that has pervaded creation since the fall and sets in motion God's redemptive plan to renew the heavens and the earth.

The bondage of decay, as Paul describes it, manifests in myriad ways—suffering, corruption, and environmental degradation. These effects of sin are not ignored in God's redemptive plan. Instead, they are addressed through the cross, which marks the beginning of the end for the forces of decay and brokenness. In Christ, God is making "all things new" (Revelation 21:5).

Hope for Creation's Liberation

The liberation of creation is tied to the redemption and glorification of the children of God. As believers experience transformation through the power of the cross, the world itself is impacted. Paul's vision is deeply holistic, emphasizing that the work of Christ not only transforms individuals but also has ripple effects that extend to communities and even the physical environment.

Dr. Desmond Ford captures this beautifully: "The cross is the centerpiece of hope, not just for humanity but for all creation. It declares that brokenness, corruption, and decay will not have the final word. Christ's victory ensures that all creation will be renewed and brought into the fullness of God's intended glory" (*The Cross and New Creation*, p. 89). This perspective reshapes how believers view the world around them. The hope of redemption is not abstract; it is a concrete promise that every aspect of life, from human relationships to the environment, will be transformed by Christ's redeeming work.

Implications for the Present Age

Understanding the cosmic scope of Christ's redemptive work has profound implications for how Christians live in the present age. The redeemed community is called to embody the values of the new creation, living in a way that anticipates and reflects the renewal promised by the cross. This includes embodying justice, compassion, stewardship, and love.

> **Justice and Compassion:** Believers are called to be agents of justice and compassion in a world marred by injustice and suffering. Charles Spurgeon once stated, "The cross compels us to love and serve, for in Christ's sacrifice we see the

ultimate act of compassion and mercy. To live in light of the cross is to reflect that same love to a broken world" (*Sermons on Christian Living*, p. 192). The cross, as the ultimate act of self-sacrificial love, motivates believers to act justly and love mercifully.

Stewardship of Creation: If the cross's redemptive work encompasses the renewal of creation, then believers are called to care for and steward the earth. This stewardship reflects God's original mandate for humanity to care for His creation (Genesis 1:28). Hauwar Stanely emphasizes, "To be a follower of Christ is to care for what He has redeemed. Creation care is not peripheral; it is central to living out the implications of the cross" (*Redemption and Creation*, p. 142). The redeemed life includes a commitment to environmental stewardship, sustainable living, and the responsible use of resources.

Holistic Transformation: Paul's vision of redemption is holistic, encompassing individual salvation, community transformation, and cosmic renewal. The cross does not merely save souls; it transforms communities and societies. Dr. Ford writes, "The power of the cross is transformative, breaking down barriers and creating a new humanity united in Christ. It is the beginning of a new creation that touches every aspect of life" (*The Transformative Power of the Cross*, p. 57).

Believers are therefore called to live as representatives of this new creation, embodying Christ's love, grace, and redemptive power in their relationships, communities, and interactions with the world around them. The cross demands that Christians engage with the world in a way that reflects God's redemptive purposes, bringing healing, justice, and restoration wherever possible.

Creation's Future Glory

Paul's depiction of creation's eager anticipation is a reminder that the story is not over. While the cross has set in motion the redemption of all things, its fullness will be realized when Christ returns and all things are brought under His lordship. The "bondage to decay" will give way to "the freedom and glory of the children of God." This future hope provides strength and motivation for believers to persevere in the present.

Charles Spurgeon captures this hope eloquently: "The cross is but the beginning of glory. In it, we see the promise of a world restored, a creation renewed, and a kingdom where righteousness dwells. Let us labor in hope, for Christ has won the victory" (*Hope Beyond the Cross*, p. 88).

Conclusion

The cross of Christ is the means by which God's redemptive plan for all creation is realized. It promises liberation from decay, renewal of all things, and transformation of individuals, communities, and the world itself. Hauwar Stanely rightly observed, "The cross is a cosmic proclamation: all things will be made new" (*The Cosmic Cross*, p. 101). As believers, we are called to live in light of this hope, embodying the values of the new creation and participating in God's work of renewal and restoration. The cross compels us to engage with the world around us, reflecting God's redemptive love and bringing His kingdom to bear in every corner of creation.

Part 2: The Power of the Cross in Human Experience

Chapter 4

"It Is Finished"

When Jesus uttered the words "It is finished" (John 19:30) from the cross, He declared the completion of His redemptive work—a work that would forever change the relationship between God and humanity. These three words are not a cry of defeat but a proclamation of victory. They signify that the purpose for which Jesus came was fully accomplished, and nothing more remains to be added. The cross stands as a beacon of hope and the assurance that salvation is secured.

The Triumph of Completion

Charles Spurgeon, in his reflections on this moment, writes, "These words were a shout of triumph, declaring that every demand of divine justice was satisfied and every sin of His people was atoned for" (*The Triumph of the Cross*, p. 57). Spurgeon's words remind us that the cross is not a mere event in history; it is the definitive act of God's redemptive plan. By proclaiming "It is finished," Jesus declared that sin's debt was fully paid and the work of salvation was complete.

The Greek word used here, *tetelestai*, was commonly used in commerce, meaning "paid in full." In the context of Jesus' sacrifice, it signifies that the debt owed by humanity due to sin was fully and irrevocably paid. There is nothing more that can or should be added. This completeness stands in stark contrast to the religious systems that require ongoing sacrifices, rituals, and works to maintain a semblance of righteousness. Jesus' declaration marks the end of striving and the beginning of rest in His finished work.

The Finality of the Cross

The cross of Christ represents the final word on salvation. There is no further sacrifice needed, no additional work to be done. In Hebrews 10:14, we read, "For by one sacrifice He has made perfect forever those who are being made holy." The cross stands as the singular, sufficient, and complete act that reconciles humanity with God. It is a declaration of the absolute sufficiency of Christ's work.

Dr. Desmond Ford captures this truth when he writes, "Calvary marked the end of religious guesswork and the beginning of assurance. The cross assures believers that their salvation is secure, their sins are forgiven, and their standing before God is complete in Christ" (*The Cross and Assurance*, p. 143). This assurance is the essence of the gospel—the good news that we are saved by grace through faith in Christ's finished work, not by our own efforts or merit.

Freedom from Religious Striving

The declaration "It is finished" liberates believers from the burden of religious striving and the fear of never measuring up. In contrast to systems that demand continual performance, Jesus' words offer a promise of rest and assurance. The cross declares that nothing more is needed; the work is complete. Paul echoes this truth in Ephesians 2:8-9: "For it is by grace you have been saved, through faith—and this is not from yourselves, it is the gift of God—not by works, so that no one can boast."

Charles Spurgeon reflects on this profound reality: "The cross is the end of all other sacrifices. No longer must we seek to atone for ourselves or earn God's favor. Christ's sacrifice is enough, and in it, we find rest" (*The Finished Work of Christ*, p. 75). This rest is not a passive state but a joyful, confident trust in what Christ has already accomplished. Believers are invited to live in the freedom and assurance that comes from knowing their salvation is secure.

The Power of Christ's Victory

In declaring "It is finished," Jesus also announced the defeat of sin, death, and the powers of darkness. Paul writes in Colossians 2:15, "Having disarmed the powers and authorities, He made a public spectacle of them, triumphing over them by the cross." The cross is the place where evil was exposed and defeated, where the power of sin was broken, and where death lost its sting. Dr. Ford emphasizes, "The cross is the place where victory was won—not by force but by self-sacrificial love. It is the ultimate triumph of grace over sin and life over death" (*Victory at Calvary*, p. 118).

Living in Light of the Finished Work

The implications of Christ's finished work are vast and transformative. Believers are called to live in the freedom and assurance that comes from knowing that their salvation is complete. This freedom is not a license to sin but a call to live in gratitude, love, and service. Paul urges believers in Galatians 5:1, "It is for freedom that Christ has set us free. Stand firm, then, and do not let yourselves be burdened again by a yoke of slavery."

Hauwar Stanely writes, "To live in the light of Christ's finished work is to live as free people—free from guilt, free from condemnation, and free to love as Christ loved us" (*Freedom and Grace*, p. 201). This freedom transforms how we see ourselves, our relationships, and our purpose in the world. We are no longer bound by fear or striving; we are invited into a relationship of grace and love with our Creator.

A New Covenant Established

The cry "It is finished" also signifies the establishment of a new covenant. The old covenant, with its rituals, sacrifices, and laws, was fulfilled and replaced by the new covenant in Christ's blood. Hebrews 8:13 states, "By calling this covenant 'new,' He has made the first one obsolete." This new covenant is characterized by grace, forgiveness, and a direct relationship with God through Christ. It is not based on external observance but on an internal transformation brought about by the Holy Spirit.

Dr. Ford elaborates, "The new covenant, sealed by Christ's blood, is a covenant of grace that brings us into intimate fellowship with God. It is the fulfillment of all God's promises and the guarantee of eternal life" (*The Covenant of Grace*, p. 150). This new reality shapes every aspect of the believer's life, leading to a deep and abiding sense of assurance and joy.

Conclusion

The cry "It is finished" is the triumphant declaration that Christ's work is complete. The cross stands as the final and sufficient word on salvation, offering freedom, assurance, and rest to all who believe. Charles Spurgeon beautifully summarizes this truth: "In the words 'It is finished,' we find the death of all our fears, the end of all our striving, and the beginning of eternal joy" (*The Triumph of the Cross*, p. 57). As believers, we are called to live in the light of this victory, confident in the finished work of Christ and free to love and serve in His name.

Chapter 5

The Fountain of Cleansing

The cross of Jesus Christ is the fountain from which flows the cleansing power of His blood—power that is foundational to the salvation of humanity. In Hebrews 9:14, the author asks, "How much more, then, will the blood of Christ, who through the eternal Spirit offered Himself unblemished to God, cleanse our consciences from acts that lead to death, so that we may serve the living God!" This verse captures the essence of the transformative and purifying nature of Christ's sacrifice. His blood does more than atone for sin; it purifies the conscience, frees believers from the burden of guilt, and empowers them to live in intimate fellowship with God.

The Cleansing Power of Christ's Blood

Throughout Scripture, blood signifies life and purity, and the shedding of blood is a powerful symbol of atonement and cleansing. In the Old Testament, the blood of sacrificial animals was used to atone for sin, but these sacrifices had to be repeated continually, and they could never fully cleanse the conscience of the worshiper (Hebrews 10:1-4). The blood of Christ, however, is different. It is a once-for-all sacrifice that cleanses completely and eternally.

Hauwar Stanely, in his treatise on sanctification, writes, "The blood of Jesus purifies not only from guilt but from the very defilement of sin, enabling believers to stand before God with a clean conscience" (*Sanctification and the Blood*, p. 221). This statement highlights a key aspect of Christ's cleansing power: it goes beyond forgiveness to bring about deep, inner purification. Through the blood of Christ, believers are not merely declared righteous—they are made clean, washed of the stains of sin, and empowered to live a new life.

A Clean Conscience: Freedom from Guilt and Shame

One of the most profound effects of Christ's cleansing blood is the purification of the conscience. Guilt and shame are powerful forces that can weigh heavily on the human soul, driving people away from God and into isolation, despair, or self-condemnation. The blood of Christ addresses this burden by washing away guilt and silencing the voice of shame. In 1 John 1:7, we read, "The blood of Jesus, His Son, purifies us from all sin." This purification is not superficial; it penetrates to the very core of our being, removing every trace of guilt and shame.

Dr. Desmond Ford emphasizes the liberating power of Christ's blood: "To be cleansed by the blood of Christ is to be set free from the chains of guilt and the accusations of the enemy. It is to know that we are fully accepted, loved, and forgiven by God" (*The Cleansing Work of the Cross*, p. 63). When believers are cleansed by the blood of Christ, they can approach God with boldness and confidence, knowing that they are truly forgiven and deeply loved.

Transformation Through Cleansing

The cleansing work of Christ's blood is transformative. It is not merely about being freed from past sins; it is about being changed from the inside out. Paul writes in 2 Corinthians 5:17, "Therefore, if anyone is in Christ, the new creation has come: The old has gone, the new is here!" The blood of Christ makes this new life possible by purifying the believer's heart and making it a dwelling place for the Holy Spirit. As the believer is cleansed, they are empowered to live a life that reflects the character and love of Christ.

Charles Spurgeon, known for his powerful sermons on the blood of Christ, proclaimed, "There is a fountain filled with blood, drawn from Emmanuel's veins; and sinners, plunged beneath that flood, lose all their guilty stains" (*The Fountain of Cleansing*, p. 89). Spurgeon's words remind us of the depth and power of Christ's cleansing work. No stain of sin is too deep, no guilt too overwhelming, for the blood of Christ to wash away.

Experiential Reflection

Countless testimonies illustrate the transformative power of Christ's cleansing blood. Throughout history, believers have experienced the profound freedom and healing that comes from being washed in His blood. Many have testified to being freed from the oppressive weight of guilt, released from the shame of their past, and empowered to live in the fullness of God's love and grace.

Consider the story of a man burdened by years of addiction and guilt. For years, he struggled to overcome his sin, feeling trapped in a cycle of defeat and shame. But when he encountered the cleansing power of Christ's blood, everything changed. He experienced forgiveness, not only intellectually but in the depths of his soul. The shame that had kept him isolated was lifted, and he was set free to live as a beloved child of God.

Dr. Ford recounts similar stories of transformation in his ministry: "Again and again, I have witnessed lives transformed by the cleansing blood of Christ. The cross does not merely forgive; it heals, restores, and empowers. It brings dead hearts to life and broken people to wholeness" (*The Transformative Power of the Blood*, p. 110).

Living in the Light of Cleansing

To be cleansed by the blood of Christ is to be called to a new way of living. It means living in the light, free from the shadows of guilt and shame. It means walking in the assurance of God's love and acceptance.

Paul writes in Hebrews 10:22, "Let us draw near to God with a sincere heart and with the full assurance that faith brings, having our hearts sprinkled to cleanse us from a guilty conscience and having our bodies washed with pure water." This invitation to draw near to God is possible because of the cleansing work of Christ's blood.

Hauwar Stanely emphasizes the call to live in light of this cleansing: "Those who have been washed by the blood of Christ are called to live as people of purity, love, and grace. They are to reflect the transformative power of the cross in every area of their lives" (*Sanctification and the Blood*, p. 225). As believers, we are called to be vessels of God's love and grace, living lives that testify to the power of Christ's cleansing work.

Conclusion

The fountain of cleansing that flows from the cross of Christ is a source of life, freedom, and transformation. Through His blood, we are washed clean, freed from guilt and shame, and empowered to live in intimate fellowship with God. As Spurgeon so beautifully expressed, "There is no stain so deep that the blood of Christ cannot cleanse. It is the fountain of hope, the wellspring of grace, and the source of all true freedom" (*The Fountain of Cleansing*, p. 89). May we live as people who have been cleansed by His blood, reflecting His love and grace to a world in need.

Chapter 6

The Healing Power of Calvary

In Isaiah 53:5, we read the profound words: "By His wounds, we are healed." This verse is a cornerstone of the Christian understanding of Christ's redemptive work on the cross, and it speaks to the depth of healing that Calvary offers. However, it is important to approach this promise with a holistic and theologically sound understanding. Unlike some religious groups who erroneously interpret this healing as an automatic guarantee of physical health or a remedy for every illness, including diseases such as cancer or chronic ailments, the biblical context reveals a more expansive and profound application. The cross extends healing to every dimension of human brokenness, but it must be understood within the broader scope of spiritual, emotional, relational, and communal renewal.

The Holistic Nature of Healing at Calvary

The healing power of Calvary reaches into every area of human life, offering restoration, wholeness, and peace. Isaiah's prophecy about the Suffering Servant points to a Messiah who would bear the sins and sufferings of humanity, providing a path to true healing and reconciliation with God. The phrase "by His wounds, we are healed" signifies far more than the alleviation of physical ailments; it encompasses the healing of the soul, freedom from the bondage of sin, and the restoration of broken relationships.

Dr. Desmond Ford emphasizes this comprehensive healing: "The wounds of Christ speak to the deepest wounds of humanity—alienation from God, the burden of guilt, and the brokenness within our hearts. The cross is the place where all of these are healed, and it extends to every aspect of our being" (*The Cross and Wholeness*, p. 132). The healing of the soul, the renewal of the mind, and the restoration of relationships are central to the promise of Calvary. This does not negate God's power to heal physically but situates physical healing within the broader framework of spiritual and relational transformation.

Christ: The Healer of Broken Hearts and Souls

Charles Spurgeon, known for his deep reflections on the healing power of Christ, captures this beautifully: "Christ is the balm for every wound, the healer of every sorrow, the mender of every heart" (*The Healing Savior*, p. 309). Spurgeon's words point to the reality that many wounds cannot be seen with human eyes. Emotional scars, deep-seated grief, broken spirits, and the pain of sin are the areas where Christ's healing touch is most profound. The cross provides healing for those who have been shattered by sin, those who carry the heavy burden of shame, and those who feel the weight of despair.

Testimonies of Transformation

The power of Calvary has transformed countless lives throughout history. Consider the story of a man burdened by addiction and broken relationships. For years, he sought healing through various means, but nothing brought true freedom. When he encountered the healing power of the cross, he experienced not only forgiveness but a deep, inner healing that led to the restoration of his relationships and the renewal of his soul. The cross reached into the darkest corners of his life, bringing light, hope, and transformation.

Similarly, a woman who had suffered years of rejection and self-hatred found healing at Calvary. The wounds inflicted by others and the lies she believed about herself were replaced by the truth of God's love and the healing touch of Christ's sacrifice. Her life was transformed as she embraced the reality that she was deeply loved, fully forgiven, and completely restored by the blood of Jesus.

Hauwar Stanely writes, "The cross addresses every human need and every human wound. It is the place where shame is silenced, guilt is erased, and new life is born. While physical healing may occur, the true power of Calvary lies in its ability to heal the human heart and restore us to wholeness" (*Healing and Redemption*, p. 198). This healing extends to relationships, communities, and every aspect of human existence, demonstrating the all-encompassing power of Christ's work on the cross.

Healing in the Context of God's Sovereign Will

While the cross has the power to bring physical healing, it is important to recognize that physical healing does not always occur in this life. The promise of healing in Isaiah 53:5 should be understood within the context of God's sovereign will and the ultimate hope of resurrection. Paul himself, despite his faith and deep relationship with Christ, experienced ongoing physical suffering (2 Corinthians 12:7-9). God's response to Paul's plea for healing was, "My grace is sufficient for you, for my power is made perfect in weakness." This underscores the truth that God's grace and strength are often made manifest in our weaknesses and sufferings, even when physical healing does not come.

Dr. Ford reflects on this dynamic: "The healing promised at Calvary is not a guarantee of a life free from suffering but a guarantee that Christ walks with us in our suffering. It is the promise of hope, renewal, and ultimate restoration in His presence" (*The Cross and Suffering*, p. 173). This perspective shifts the focus from seeking physical healing as a measure of faith to trusting in God's presence and redemptive purposes in every circumstance.

The Healing Community

The cross not only heals individuals but also calls believers into a community of healing and restoration. The church is to be a place where the healing power of Christ is made manifest through love, support, forgiveness, and the sharing of burdens. Paul's exhortation to "bear one another's burdens" (Galatians 6:2) is a reflection of the healing work of Calvary lived out in the body of Christ. In community, believers find support, encouragement, and the tangible expression of Christ's healing love.

Conclusion

The healing power of Calvary extends to every dimension of human brokenness—spiritual, emotional, relational, and even physical. While physical healing may occur, the true promise of the cross is a deeper, more comprehensive healing that transforms the soul, renews the mind, and restores broken lives. Charles Spurgeon's words remind us that "Christ is the balm for every wound, the healer of every sorrow, the mender of every heart" (*The Healing Savior*, p. 309). As we embrace the healing power of the cross, we are invited to experience wholeness, freedom, and the transforming love of Christ in every aspect of our lives. May we live as people who have been healed by the wounds of Christ, offering His love and grace to a broken world in need of healing.

Part 3: The Incomparable Jesus

Chapter 7

Jesus: The Fulfillment of God's Promises

The entirety of Scripture is a grand narrative that points to the fulfillment of God's promises, all of which converge in the person and work of Jesus Christ. The Apostle Paul encapsulates this truth in 2 Corinthians 1:20, "For no matter how many promises God has made, they are 'Yes' in Christ." This powerful declaration reveals that every promise, every covenant, every prophetic word finds its ultimate realization and consummation in Jesus. He is not merely one aspect of God's redemptive plan; He is its fulfillment, its culmination, and its glorious climax.

The Fulfillment of Every Covenant Promise

Throughout the Old Testament, God established covenants with His people, each containing promises that pointed to a greater fulfillment. The covenant with Abraham promised blessing to all nations through his offspring (Genesis 12:3). The covenant with Moses established the law, revealing God's standard of holiness and humanity's need for a Redeemer. The covenant with David promised an everlasting kingdom (2 Samuel 7:12-16). Each of these covenants, while significant in their own right, pointed beyond themselves to something greater—someone greater—who would fulfill all that they foreshadowed.

Jesus is that fulfillment. He is the true seed of Abraham through whom all nations are blessed (Galatians 3:16). He is the perfect fulfillment of the law, living a sinless life and offering Himself as the perfect sacrifice for sin (Matthew 5:17). He is the Son of David who reigns eternally as King of Kings and Lord of Lords (Luke 1:32-33). Dr. Desmond Ford captures this beautifully: "In Christ, all the promises of God are brought to their ultimate fulfillment, making Him the anchor of our hope" (*Christ Our Anchor*, p. 88). Jesus embodies the faithfulness of God, demonstrating that every word spoken by God is trustworthy and true.

The "Yes" and "Amen" of God

When Paul writes that all of God's promises are "Yes" in Christ, he underscores the certainty and assurance that believers have in Jesus. The phrase "Yes" speaks to the fulfillment of God's promises, while "Amen" (meaning "so be it" or "truly") reflects the affirmation and guarantee of what God has accomplished through Christ. This means that every promise God has ever made is realized and affirmed in Jesus. There is no promise left unfulfilled; there is no covenant left incomplete.

Charles Spurgeon, reflecting on this truth, stated, "Christ is God's grand 'Yes' to all that He has spoken. Every promise made by God finds its seal and its completion in the person of His Son. There is no half-measure in God's faithfulness; all is complete in Christ" (*The Promises of God Fulfilled*, p. 173). For believers, this means that we can approach God with confidence, knowing that His promises are as certain as the finished work of Christ on the cross.

The Meritorious Work of Christ on the Cross

The fulfillment of God's promises is rooted in the meritorious work of Christ on the cross. It is through His life, death, and resurrection that the promises of God are secured and applied to His people. Jesus' sacrifice on the cross was not merely a demonstration of God's love; it was the means by which every promise was made effective. By His wounds, we are healed (Isaiah 53:5). By His blood, we are redeemed (Ephesians 1:7). By His resurrection, we have the hope of eternal life (1 Corinthians 15:20-22). Every blessing, every grace, every aspect of salvation is made possible because of what Christ accomplished on the cross.

Dr. Ford emphasizes this central truth: "The cross is the anchor of all hope because it is the place where every promise of God is secured. There, Christ bore the weight of sin, fulfilled the righteous demands of the law, and opened the way for every blessing to flow to those who believe" (*The Cross and God's Promises*, p. 112). The cross is not merely a symbol of suffering; it is the glorious demonstration of God's faithfulness and the source of every spiritual blessing.

The Promise of Redemption and Restoration

One of the greatest promises fulfilled in Christ is the promise of redemption and restoration. From the moment sin entered the world, God promised a Redeemer who would crush the serpent's head (Genesis 3:15). This promise, known as the "protoevangelium," finds its fulfillment in Jesus, who defeated sin, death, and the devil through His death and resurrection. The redemption He provides is comprehensive, encompassing not only forgiveness of sins but also the restoration of all that was lost and broken.

Hauwar Stanely writes, "In Christ, God's promise of redemption is not limited to the forgiveness of sins. It extends to the renewal of hearts, the reconciliation of relationships, and the restoration of all creation. Jesus is the fulfillment of every promise of life and hope" (*Redemption and Fulfillment*, p. 209). This means that the work of Christ on the cross touches every aspect of life, bringing healing, hope, and renewal to individuals, communities, and the world.

The Assurance of God's Faithfulness

The fulfillment of God's promises in Christ gives believers unshakable assurance. Because Jesus has fulfilled every promise, we can trust that

God's Word is true and that His purposes will be accomplished. This assurance is not based on human effort or circumstances but on the finished work of Christ. As Paul writes in Romans 8:32, "He who did not spare His own Son, but gave Him up for us all—how will He not also, along with Him, graciously give us all things?" The cross is the guarantee of God's faithfulness and the anchor of our hope.

Spurgeon captures this assurance when he declares, "God's promises are as sure as the blood of His Son. If Christ has secured it, then it is ours, and nothing in heaven or on earth can take it away" (*The Certainty of God's Promises*, p. 188). This is the confidence that believers carry—the knowledge that every promise is secure in Christ and that nothing can separate us from His love.

Living in the Light of Fulfillment

Because Jesus is the fulfillment of God's promises, believers are called to live in the light of that fulfillment. This means living with confidence, hope, and joy, knowing that God's purposes are being accomplished and that His promises are sure. It means trusting in His provision, relying on His strength, and walking in His grace. It also means being agents of His promise to the world, reflecting His love, grace, and truth in every sphere of life.

Conclusion

Jesus is the culmination of God's redemptive plan, the fulfillment of every covenant promise, and the assurance of every blessing. In Him, all of God's promises are "Yes" and "Amen." As Dr. Ford notes, "In Christ, all the promises of God are brought to their ultimate fulfillment, making Him the anchor of our hope" (*Christ Our Anchor*, p. 88). The cross stands as the meritorious and glorious work through which every promise is secured, every hope is realized, and every believer is assured of God's unchanging faithfulness. May we live in the light of this fulfillment, anchored in the hope and grace of our Lord Jesus Christ.

Chapter 8

The Incomparable Christ

Who is this man? Born in the most unusual of circumstances, Jesus of Nazareth entered the world in a humble stable, surrounded by animals, to a young, unmarried woman and a carpenter in an obscure town. His birth troubled kings and stirred fear in the powerful, yet He had no political army or ambition. As a child, He confounded the wise teachers in the temple, and as an adult, He transformed lives through simple acts of compassion, healing the sick without any medical training and speaking words that pierced hearts. He wrote no books, and yet more volumes have been written about Him than any other figure in history. Countless songs and hymns have been composed in His honor, yet He never penned a single one. Who is this man?

The Humility of Christ

Jesus' humility is unparalleled. Though He was in very nature God, He "did not consider equality with God something to be used to His own advantage; rather, He made Himself nothing by taking the very nature of a servant, being made in human likeness" (Philippians 2:6-7). The King of Kings chose to come into the world in poverty and obscurity, living a life that defied expectations of power and glory. In an age where rulers displayed their might through military conquests and grand palaces, Jesus revealed His kingship through acts of service and self-sacrifice. He washed the feet of His disciples, touched the untouchable, and welcomed the outcast.

Charles Spurgeon captures this astounding humility, saying, "There is no one like Christ. His love surpasses knowledge, His mercy endures forever, and His sacrifice covers all" (*The Character of Christ*, p. 97). Jesus' humility was not weakness; it was strength under perfect control. It was the humility of a King who could have summoned legions of angels yet chose to surrender Himself to the cross out of love for humanity.

The Sacrifice of Christ

The cross of Christ stands at the heart of His incomparable nature. Jesus did not simply come to teach or heal—He came to give His life as a ransom for many (Mark 10:45). His sacrificial death on the cross was the ultimate expression of love and the fulfillment of His mission. Through His suffering, He bore the weight of the world's sin, reconciling humanity to God and providing a path to salvation for all who believe.

Dr. Desmond Ford reflects on the significance of Christ's sacrifice: "No one else could bear the weight of humanity's guilt and conquer death itself. In His sacrifice, Jesus showed the depth of divine love and the unfathomable cost of our redemption" (*The Cross and Redemption*, p. 72). The sacrifice of Christ is incomparable because it is both unique and universally sufficient. It is the work of a Savior who loves without limit, giving Himself completely for the sake of those He came to save.

The Love of Christ

At the heart of Jesus' life and ministry is His unparalleled love. The Gospels are filled with accounts of Jesus' compassion and mercy. He touched the leper, healed the blind, fed the hungry, and raised the dead. He extended grace to the sinner, mercy to the broken, and hope to the despairing. He crossed social, cultural, and religious boundaries to reach those whom society had rejected.

Paul writes in Ephesians 3:18-19, "I pray that you... may have power, together with all the Lord's holy people, to grasp how wide and long and high and deep is the love of Christ, and to know this love that surpasses knowledge." Jesus' love is incomparable because it surpasses human understanding. It is a love that forgives seventy times seven, that seeks the lost, and that lays down its life for its friends.

Spurgeon declared, "There is no one like Christ. His love surpasses knowledge, His mercy endures forever, and His sacrifice covers all" (*The Character of Christ*, p. 97). This love is not abstract or theoretical; it is deeply personal and transformative. It is the love that pursued the lost sheep, welcomed the prodigal, and forgave those who crucified Him.

A Man Who Troubled Kings and Comforted the Broken

From the moment of His birth, Jesus disturbed the status quo. King Herod sought to kill Him, fearing the prophecy of a newborn King who would challenge his rule (Matthew 2:1-16). Throughout His ministry, religious leaders plotted against Him, unsettled by His teachings that exposed their hypocrisy and called for true righteousness. Jesus did not seek political power, yet His presence challenged the powerful and brought hope to the oppressed.

While He troubled kings, Jesus comforted the brokenhearted. He said, "Come to me, all you who are weary and burdened, and I will give you rest" (Matthew 11:28). The same man who spoke with authority and silenced storms also wept at the tomb of His friend Lazarus (John 11:35). His compassion was not a show; it was the essence of who He is. Jesus entered into the pain of humanity, offering comfort, healing, and hope.

The Transformative Impact of Christ

Jesus' influence on human history is unmatched. Millions of lives have been transformed by His message and His sacrifice. Entire civilizations have been shaped by His teachings on love, justice, mercy, and forgiveness. Countless individuals have found hope, healing, and purpose in Him. Books and songs have been written to honor Him, and His words continue to resonate with power across generations.

Hauwar Stanely writes, "The life and teachings of Christ have reshaped the course of history. His influence transcends time and culture, touching every aspect of human existence. He is not simply a figure of history; He is the Savior of the world" (*The Impact of Christ*, p. 104). Jesus' life, death, and resurrection have left an indelible mark on the world, one that cannot be erased or forgotten.

The Incomparable Nature of Christ

Jesus is incomparable in every way. His humility, sacrifice, and love stand as a beacon of light in a dark world. He is the fulfillment of every promise, the embodiment of God's love, and the Savior who gave everything for us. There is no one like Him. He is the King who reigns through service, the Shepherd who lays down His life for the sheep, and the Lord who calls us into a relationship of grace and love.

Charles Spurgeon's words ring true: "There is no one like Christ. His love surpasses knowledge, His mercy endures forever, and His sacrifice covers all" (*The Character of Christ*, p. 97). Jesus Christ is the one who troubled kings and comforted the broken, who healed without medicine, and who spoke with authority yet walked in humility. He is the one who has transformed hearts and reshaped history. He is our Savior, our Redeemer, and our King—the incomparable Christ.

Chapter 9

The Victorious King

The resurrection and exaltation of Jesus Christ stand as the ultimate demonstration of His victory over sin, death, and every power that opposes the reign of God. The Apostle Paul, in his powerful Christological hymn, writes, "And being found in appearance as a man, He humbled Himself by becoming obedient to death—even death on a cross! Therefore God exalted Him to the highest place and gave Him the name that is above every name, that at the name of Jesus every knee should bow, in heaven and on earth and under the earth, and every tongue acknowledge that Jesus Christ is Lord, to the glory of God the Father" (Philippians 2:8-11). The cross was not the end; it was the pathway to victory and exaltation. Jesus, the crucified Savior, is now the victorious King, reigning in glory.

The Resurrection: Christ's Triumph Over Death

The resurrection of Jesus Christ is the linchpin of the Christian faith. It is the definitive proof that sin and death have been defeated. Paul declares in 1 Corinthians 15:17, "If Christ has not been raised, your faith is futile; you are still in your sins." But Christ **has** been raised, and His resurrection guarantees not only our justification but also the defeat of the powers of darkness.

Dr. Desmond Ford writes, "The resurrection is the victory cry of Christ over the grave. It is the declaration that sin, death, and Satan have no hold over those who are in Him. Through His resurrection, Jesus has broken the power of death and opened the way to eternal life" (*The Resurrection and Our Hope*, p. 56). The empty tomb is a symbol of hope, a reminder that death does not have the final word, and a promise of the believer's future resurrection.

The resurrection also validates every claim Jesus made about Himself. He is not merely a teacher or prophet; He is the Son of God, with power over life and death. When He rose from the dead, He proved beyond a shadow of a doubt that He is the victorious King, the One who has conquered every enemy.

Exaltation to the Highest Place

Paul's words in Philippians 2:9-11 reveal the magnitude of Christ's exaltation: "Therefore God exalted Him to the highest place and gave Him the name that is above every name." Jesus' exaltation is not simply a reward for His obedience; it is the rightful acknowledgment of His divine identity and victorious work. He now reigns as Lord of all, and every knee will bow and every tongue confess His lordship.

Charles Spurgeon, in his reflections on the exaltation of Christ, states, "The risen Christ is no longer the man of sorrows; He is the King of glory. He is crowned with honor and majesty, adored by angels and worshipped by His redeemed. In His exaltation, we see the triumph of grace and the assurance of our salvation" (*The Exalted Savior*, p. 210). This exaltation is not a distant reality; it is a present truth. Jesus reigns now, and His victory is the foundation of our hope and confidence.

The Guarantor of Our Salvation

Christ's victory is not an isolated event; it has direct implications for every believer. As the victorious King, Jesus is the guarantor of our salvation. His resurrection and exaltation ensure that the work He began will be brought to completion. Paul writes in Romans 8:34, "Who then is the one who condemns? No one. Christ Jesus who died—more than that, who was raised to life—is at the right hand of

God and is also interceding for us." The exalted Christ intercedes for His people, ensuring that nothing can separate us from the love of God.

Hauwar Stanely writes, "The exaltation of Christ is the believer's assurance. He reigns not as a distant King but as an Advocate, a Shepherd, and a Savior who actively works on behalf of His people" (*Christ the King and Advocate*, p. 155). This means that every victory Christ won—over sin, death, and the powers of darkness—is shared with His people. Believers live not as defeated people but as those who share in the triumph of their King.

The Cosmic Victory of Christ

The victory of Christ extends beyond individual salvation; it encompasses all of creation. Paul writes in Colossians 1:19-20, "For God was pleased to have all His fullness dwell in Him, and through Him to reconcile to Himself all things, whether things on earth or things in heaven, by making peace through His blood, shed on the cross." The reign of Christ as the victorious King signals the beginning of cosmic restoration. Every broken thing will be made new, every injustice will be made right, and every enemy will be put under His feet.

Dr. Ford emphasizes the cosmic scope of Christ's victory: "The cross and resurrection are not merely historical events; they are the axis upon which the cosmos turns. In Christ's victory, all creation finds hope and the promise of renewal" (*Cosmic Redemption in Christ*, p. 184). This victory is both a present reality and a future hope. While we live in a world still marred by sin and brokenness, we do so with the assurance that the final victory has already been won.

The Hope of Every Believer

The resurrection and exaltation of Christ give every believer a reason to hope. Because He lives, we too will live (John 14:19). Because He reigns, we can face every trial, every sorrow, and every challenge with confidence. Paul's words in 1 Corinthians 15:57 remind us, "But thanks be to God! He gives us the victory through our Lord Jesus Christ." This victory is not earned by our efforts; it is a gift of grace, secured by the victorious King.

Charles Spurgeon captures the hope of the believer: "The risen Christ is our guarantee that no power in hell or earth can prevail against us. In His victory, we find our strength, our hope, and our assurance" (*The Victory of the King*, p. 121). This is the hope that sustains believers in every circumstance—the knowledge that Christ has conquered and that His victory is our victory.

Living Under the Reign of the Victorious King

To acknowledge Christ as the victorious King is to live under His reign. It means submitting every aspect of our lives to His lordship, trusting in His power, and walking in His victory. It means living with courage, hope, and a deep sense of purpose. Paul writes in Ephesians 1:22-23 that God "placed all things under His feet and appointed Him to be head over everything for the church, which is His body." As members of His body, we are called to live as ambassadors of His kingdom, reflecting His victory in how we love, serve, and proclaim His name.

Conclusion

The resurrection and exaltation of Christ declare that He is the victorious King, the One who has conquered sin, death, and every power of darkness. He reigns as Lord, interceding for His people and guaranteeing their salvation. As Dr. Ford notes, "The victorious King is our assurance and our hope. In Him, we see the triumph of grace and the fulfillment of every promise" (*The Victorious Christ*, p. 193).

May we live in the light of His victory, confident in His reign, and ever proclaiming the hope we have in our risen and exalted King.

Part 4: Living in the Light of the Cross

Chapter 10

The Call to Grateful Living

The grace of Christ, demonstrated through His sacrificial death on the cross, calls forth a response of deep gratitude from all who have experienced its transformative power. Gratitude is not merely an emotion; it is a way of life—a posture of the heart that reflects a profound recognition of what Christ has done. As Paul exhorts in Colossians 3:17, "Whatever you do, whether in word or deed, do it all in the name of the Lord Jesus, giving thanks to God the Father through Him." This call to gratitude is a call to live every aspect of life in light of the grace of Calvary, acknowledging that everything we are and have is a gift from the Savior.

The Depth of Christ's Mercy and the Call to Respond

The mercy of Christ is unmatched. He came as the Lamb, bearing the sins of the world and offering Himself as the perfect sacrifice for our redemption. But we must also remember that He will return as the Lion, not to plead but to bring all things to completion and usher in a new reality. This truth should awaken in us both reverent awe and deep gratitude. Dr. Desmond Ford writes, "To live in the shadow of the cross is to remember that mercy and judgment are inextricably intertwined in the person of Christ. His first coming brought mercy; His second coming will bring the culmination of all things" (*The Cross and the Kingdom*, p. 142). Gratitude flows from an understanding that we live in a moment of grace, awaiting the return of our victorious King.

Charles Spurgeon captures the essence of gratitude, saying, "Gratitude is the echo of grace in the soul. When we truly understand what Christ has done, gratitude is not an option; it is the only response worthy of such love" (*Living in the Light of Grace*, p. 201). The mercy of Christ compels us to live lives marked by thanksgiving, humility, and service.

Practical Application: Living a Life of Gratitude

Gratitude is not passive; it is active and transformative. It shapes how we think, how we speak, and how we act. The believer's life is marked by gratitude, love, and service, reflecting the transformative power of the cross.

Gratitude in Our Words and Actions

Paul's exhortation in Colossians 3:17 calls believers to do everything "in the name of the Lord Jesus, giving thanks." This means that gratitude should permeate every word we speak and every action we take. Our interactions with others should reflect the grace we have received. Hauwar Stanely writes, "The grateful heart speaks differently, acts differently, and loves differently because it has been touched by the mercy of Christ. Gratitude transforms the mundane into acts of worship" (*Gratitude and Grace*, p. 98).

Gratitude Expressed Through Love

Gratitude is not self-contained; it overflows in love for others. Just as Christ loved us and gave Himself for us, we are called to love others with the same selfless love. This love is expressed in acts of kindness, compassion, and forgiveness. Paul writes in Ephesians 5:1-2, "Follow God's example, therefore, as dearly loved children and walk in the way of love, just as Christ loved us and gave Himself up for us as a fragrant offering and sacrifice to God." Gratitude moves us to love sacrificially, reflecting the love we have received.

Gratitude in Service

A grateful heart is a serving heart. Jesus modeled servant leadership by washing the feet of His disciples and giving His life for others. Gratitude compels us to serve others, not out of obligation, but out of a deep desire to reflect Christ's love. Dr. Ford emphasizes, "Service is the natural outflow of a heart that has been touched by grace. When we recognize what Christ has done for us, we cannot help but extend that grace to others through acts of service" (*The Grateful Heart and the Servant Life*, p. 78).

Gratitude in Times of Trial

Living a life of gratitude does not mean that we are exempt from trials and suffering. In fact, it is often in the midst of difficulties that gratitude becomes most powerful. Paul, who endured countless hardships, wrote, "Give thanks in all circumstances; for this is God's will for you in Christ Jesus" (1 Thessalonians 5:18). Gratitude in difficult times is a testament to the transformative power of the cross. It declares that our hope is not in our circumstances but in the One who holds all things in His hands.

Charles Spurgeon observed, "True gratitude is not dependent on the sunshine of prosperity; it thrives in the storms of adversity. When we remember the cross, we find reason to be thankful even in the darkest of days" (*Gratitude in the Storm*, p. 67). This kind of gratitude is a witness to the world of the sufficiency of Christ's grace.

Remembering the Mercies of Christ

The call to grateful living is rooted in the remembrance of Christ's mercies. We must continually remind ourselves of who He is and what He has done. He came as the Lamb, offering Himself for our sins. He will return as the Lion, bringing justice and renewing all things. This dual reality shapes our gratitude and reminds us of the urgency of living for His glory. Hauwar Stanely writes, "To remember Christ's mercy is to live with a sense of awe and urgency. Gratitude is not a mere feeling; it is a lifestyle that reflects the glory of the cross" (*Living in Light of the Cross*, p. 133).

A New Beginning in Grateful Reality

The return of Christ will mark the end of the old order and the beginning of a new reality. All things will be made new, and we will see Him face to face. Until that day, we are called to live in the light of His mercy, offering our lives as a testimony to His grace. Gratitude fuels this mission, reminding us that every moment is an opportunity to reflect the love, grace, and mercy of our Savior.

Conclusion

Gratitude is the natural response to the grace of Calvary. It shapes every aspect of our lives, from our words and actions to our love and service. As Paul exhorts in Colossians 3:17, "Whatever you do... do it all in the name of the Lord Jesus, giving thanks to God the Father through Him." The mercy of Christ compels us to live with hearts full of thanksgiving, reflecting His love to the world and living in anticipation of His return as the victorious Lion who will bring all things to their fulfillment. May we live lives of grateful worship, ever mindful of the grace we have received and the hope we have in Christ.

The cross of Jesus Christ is the ultimate demonstration of selfless, sacrificial, and unconditional love. It is the standard by which all love is measured and the call to action for every believer. The Apostle Paul exhorts us in Ephesians 5:2, "Walk in love, as Christ loved us and gave Himself up for us as a fragrant offering and sacrifice to God." This call to walk in love is not theoretical or abstract—it is a call to embody the love of Christ in every aspect of our lives, especially in the face of human suffering, injustice, and brokenness. In a world filled with hunger, war, genocide, and social injustices, the cross demands that we cannot remain bystanders. We must be agents of Christ's love and grace, responding to God's interruptions in our daily lives with compassion and action.

Selfless Love in the Face of Injustice

At the heart of the cross is selfless love—a love that places the needs of others above our own, even when it costs us greatly. Jesus did not come to be served but to serve and to give His life as a ransom for many (Mark 10:45). His entire life and ministry were marked by interruptions—moments when He chose to stop, listen, and act in compassion. Whether it was healing the sick, feeding the hungry, or speaking to the marginalized, Jesus consistently demonstrated that true love is selfless and responsive to human suffering.

Dr. Desmond Ford emphasizes, "The cross is God's interruption of human history. It is His declaration that love does not stand idly by in the face of suffering but enters into it, bearing its weight and offering hope" (*The Cross and Human Suffering*, p. 98). As followers of Christ, we must be aware of the "interruptions" God places in our paths—opportunities to love and serve others, even when it is inconvenient or challenging. To walk in the way of the cross is to be willing to lay down our own plans, comfort, and desires for the sake of others.

Sacrificial Love: A Call to Action

The love of Christ is sacrificial, as demonstrated on the cross where He gave His life for the salvation of humanity. Paul reminds us that Christ "gave Himself up for us" (Ephesians 5:2), setting the standard for what it means to love sacrificially. This love calls us to move beyond words and to act, particularly in the face of social injustices, poverty, and violence. We cannot turn a blind eye to the suffering around us; we must be willing to step into difficult and even dangerous situations to bring hope, justice, and healing.

Charles Spurgeon spoke of this sacrificial love, saying, "True love does not count the cost. It gives of itself wholly, even when the sacrifice is great. The cross is the measure of this love, and we are called to follow in its path" (*The Sacrificial Life*, p. 150). This sacrificial love compels us to confront systems of oppression, to care for the marginalized, and to advocate for those who have no voice. The cross is not a passive symbol; it is a call to active, self-giving love in a broken world.

Unconditional Love Amid Human Brokenness

The cross of Christ also reveals the unconditional nature of His love. Jesus did not wait for humanity to be worthy or deserving; He loved us while we were still sinners (Romans 5:8). His love extends to the unlovable, the rejected, and the broken. In a world marked by division, hatred, and violence, the cross calls us to love without condition. This means loving those who are different from us, those who have wronged us, and even those who may be considered our enemies.

Hauwar Stanely writes, "The unconditional love of Christ displayed on the cross leaves no room for indifference. It compels us to see every human being as one for whom Christ died and to love them with the same passion and grace" (*The Boundless Love of God*, p. 132).

When we encounter human suffering, whether through war, genocide, poverty, or social injustice, we cannot stand by. The love of the cross calls us to enter into the pain of others and to be agents of healing and reconciliation.

Responding to God's Interruptions

God often interrupts our lives with opportunities to demonstrate the love of Christ. These interruptions may come in the form of a neighbor in need, a social injustice that demands our attention, or a crisis that requires our resources and time. To walk in love as Christ did means being attentive to these divine interruptions and responding with compassion, courage, and selflessness. We cannot claim to follow the way of the cross while ignoring the suffering and injustices that surround us.

Dr. Ford reflects on this dynamic: "Every act of injustice, every cry of the oppressed, and every broken heart is a call to the people of God to act. The cross is not a relic of the past; it is a living call to engage with the suffering of the world with the love and power of Christ" (*The Cross and Social Justice*, p. 165). This means standing against systems that perpetuate violence and poverty, advocating for those who are voiceless, and extending the love of Christ to all, regardless of the cost.

Practical Expressions of Cross-Centered Love

To live out the love of the cross, believers must engage in practical acts of service and compassion. This love is not theoretical; it is lived out in concrete ways that bring healing and hope to a hurting world.

Advocacy for the Oppressed

The love of Christ compels us to speak out against injustice and to advocate for those who are marginalized and oppressed. Paul's call to "walk in love" means standing with those who suffer and using our voices, resources, and influence to bring about change. Charles Spurgeon reminds us, "Love that does not act is no love at all. The cross calls us to stand with the oppressed and to be the hands and feet of Christ in a world that so desperately needs His touch" (*Love in Action*, p. 77).

Compassion for the Suffering

Jesus' ministry was marked by compassion for the suffering. He healed the sick, fed the hungry, and comforted the sorrowful. As His followers, we are called to show the same compassion. This may mean volunteering at a shelter, providing for the needs of a struggling family, or simply listening to someone's pain. Hauwar Stanely writes, "Compassion is the heart of the cross. It moves us beyond sympathy to action, beyond words to deeds" (*Compassionate Living*, p. 89).

Peacemaking in Times of Conflict

The cross is a symbol of reconciliation. Jesus made peace between God and humanity through His sacrifice, and He calls us to be peacemakers in a world of conflict and division. Paul writes in 2 Corinthians 5:18-19 that God has given us the ministry of reconciliation. This means working to bring peace in our communities, standing against violence, and seeking to heal divisions.

Conclusion

The cross is the standard by which we measure all love—selfless, sacrificial, and unconditional. In a world filled with suffering, hunger, war, genocide, and social injustices, we are called to be more than bystanders. We must be agents of Christ's love, responding to God's interruptions with courage, compassion, and a willingness to sacrifice. As Charles Spurgeon so powerfully declared, "The cross compels us to love without limits, to serve without hesitation, and to enter the suffering of the world with the hope of Christ" (*The Cross and the Call to Love*, p. 103). May we walk in the way of the cross, loving as Christ loved, and bringing His light to a world in need.

Chapter 12

The Hope of Glory

The cross of Jesus Christ is not only the symbol of suffering and sacrifice but also the guarantee of future glory for every believer. In Romans 8:18, the Apostle Paul declares, "I consider that our present sufferings are not worth comparing with the glory that will be revealed in us." This profound statement captures the eschatological hope rooted in the cross. The pain, trials, and hardships of this present life pale in comparison to the glorious future that awaits those who are in Christ. It is the hope of glory that sustains, inspires, and empowers believers to persevere through all of life's challenges.

The Cross as the Guarantee of Future Glory

The cross is not merely a moment in history; it is the axis upon which the believer's hope turns. Through the death and resurrection of Jesus, a new reality has been inaugurated—a reality in which death is defeated, sin is conquered, and a glorious future is assured. Paul writes in 1 Corinthians 15:20-22, "But Christ has indeed been raised from the dead, the firstfruits of those who have fallen asleep. For since death came through a man, the resurrection of the dead comes also through a man. For as in Adam all die, so in Christ all will be made alive."

Dr. Desmond Ford emphasizes the connection between the cross and future glory: "The cross is not only the place where sin was defeated; it is the gateway to a new creation. It points us to a glorious future where suffering will cease, and God's reign will be fully realized" (*The Cross and Future Glory*, p. 256). The resurrection of Jesus is the firstfruits of what is to come—the promise that all who belong to Him will share in His victory and glory.

Eschatological Implications of the Cross

The hope of glory has profound eschatological implications. It speaks of a future where God will wipe away every tear, where death and suffering will be no more, and where His reign of justice and peace will be fully established. Paul captures this hope in Romans 8:21 when he writes that creation itself "will be liberated from its bondage to decay and brought into the freedom and glory of the children of God." The cross is the assurance that this future is not merely a distant dream but a guaranteed reality.

Charles Spurgeon reflects on this eschatological hope, saying, "The cross has turned the night of death into the dawn of eternal glory. Every wound He bore was a victory, and every drop of His blood was a promise of the life to come" (*The Cross and Eternal Hope*, p. 112). Spurgeon's words remind us that the cross is not only the means by which we are saved but also the pledge of our future inheritance in Christ.

Perseverance in the Face of Suffering

The hope of glory inspires perseverance, courage, and faithfulness in the midst of suffering. Paul's declaration that "our present sufferings are not worth comparing with the glory that will be revealed in us" (Romans 8:18) is a reminder that the trials we face are temporary and pale in comparison to the eternal glory that awaits us. This hope does not minimize our suffering but places it in the context of God's redemptive plan. It gives us the strength to endure, knowing that our suffering is not in vain.

Dr. Ford writes, "The cross reminds us that suffering is not the end of the story. It points us forward to a day when all things will be made new, when every tear will be wiped away, and when the glory of God will fill the earth" (*The Cross and Perseverance*, p. 189). This hope is not mere optimism; it is rooted in the historical reality of the resurrection and the promises of God.

The Transformative Power of Hope

The hope of glory is transformative. It changes how we live in the present because it reminds us of our ultimate destiny. Paul writes in Philippians 3:20-21, "But our citizenship is in heaven. And we eagerly await a Savior from there, the Lord Jesus Christ, who, by the power that enables Him to bring everything under His control, will transform our lowly bodies so that they will be like His glorious body." This hope gives believers a new perspective on life, encouraging us to live with purpose, faithfulness, and a focus on eternal things.

Hauwar Stanely captures this transformative power: "The hope of glory reshapes our priorities, strengthens our resolve, and fills us with courage. It reminds us that we are not living for this world alone but for a kingdom that cannot be shaken" (*Living in Hope*, p. 214). As believers, we are called to live as people of hope, reflecting the light of Christ in a dark world and pointing others to the glory that is to come.

Living in Light of Future Glory

To live in the hope of glory is to live with a sense of anticipation and purpose. It means that our lives are marked by faithfulness, love, and a commitment to the mission of Christ. We are called to be ambassadors of His kingdom, proclaiming the good news of the cross and living out its transformative power. Paul's exhortation in 1 Corinthians 15:58 captures this call: "Therefore, my dear brothers and sisters, stand firm. Let nothing move you. Always give yourselves fully to the work of the Lord, because you know that your labor in the Lord is not in vain."

Charles Spurgeon encourages believers to live in this hope, saying, "The cross points us to a future that is secure, a glory that is certain, and a hope that cannot be shaken. Let us live with courage, faith, and a heart full of gratitude, for the best is yet to come" (*The Hope of Glory*, p. 175). This hope empowers us to face trials with confidence, to serve others with love, and to persevere in the faith, knowing that our labor is not in vain.

The Ultimate Victory of Christ

The hope of glory is rooted in the ultimate victory of Christ. He is the victorious King who will return to establish His reign fully and completely. Revelation 21:4-5 gives us a glimpse of this future: "He will wipe every tear from their eyes. There will be no more death or mourning or crying or pain, for the old order of things has passed away. He who was seated on the throne said, 'I am making everything new!'" This is the hope that sustains us—the promise that one day, all things will be made right.

Dr. Ford writes, "The cross is the guarantee of the final victory. It is the assurance that the kingdom of God will prevail, that evil will be defeated, and that every promise of God will be fulfilled" (*The Victory of the Cross*, p. 222). This hope is not wishful thinking; it is a certainty grounded in the person and work of Jesus Christ.

Conclusion

The cross is the guarantee of future glory. It points us to a glorious future where suffering will cease, and God's reign will be fully realized. As Paul writes in Romans 8:18, "I consider that our present sufferings are not worth comparing with the glory that will be revealed in us." This hope inspires perseverance, courage, and faithfulness, reminding us that the best is yet to come. May we live as people of hope, anchored in the promise of the cross and eagerly awaiting the day when we will see our Savior face to face in all His glory. As Charles Spurgeon so beautifully expressed, "The cross leads to the crown, and every tear we shed on the journey will be wiped away in the light of His glory" (*The Glory That Awaits*, p. 139).

Conclusion: Thanks to Calvary

The cross of Christ transforms everything—cosmic order, human hearts, and eternal destinies. It is both the foundation and the pinnacle of the Christian life. Through the cross, sin is defeated, reconciliation is accomplished, and hope is assured. As Dr. Desmond Ford so powerfully wrote, "The cross is where all of God's promises converge and where our future is secured. It is the place where love triumphed over judgment, offering us the assurance of God's unending grace" (*The Triumph of the Cross*, p. 267). "Thanks to Calvary" calls every believer to embrace the full implications of Christ's finished work with deep gratitude, unshakable confidence, and living hope. The cross changes everything—and because of it, we live transformed lives for His glory.

Appendix

A. Key Pauline Texts on the Cross

The Apostle Paul's writings emphasize the centrality of the cross in Christian faith and theology. Below is a compilation of key Pauline texts that highlight the significance, purpose, and transformative power of the cross.

1. Romans 3:23-25

"For all have sinned and fall short of the glory of God, and all are justified freely by his grace through the redemption that came by Christ Jesus. God presented Christ as a sacrifice of atonement, through the shedding of his blood—to be received by faith."

2. Romans 5:8

"But God demonstrates his own love for us in this: While we were still sinners, Christ died for us."

3. Romans 6:6-7

"For we know that our old self was crucified with him so that the body ruled by sin might be done away with, that we should no longer be slaves to sin—because anyone who has died has been set free from sin."

4. Romans 8:1-2

"Therefore, there is now no condemnation for those who are in Christ Jesus, because through Christ Jesus the law of the Spirit who gives life has set you free from the law of sin and death."

5. Romans 8:32

"He who did not spare his own Son, but gave him up for us all—how will he not also, along with him, graciously give us all things?"

6. 1 Corinthians 1:18

"For the message of the cross is foolishness to those who are perishing, but to us who are being saved it is the power of God."

7. 1 Corinthians 2:2

"For I resolved to know nothing while I was with you except Jesus Christ and him crucified."

8. 1 Corinthians 15:3-4

"For what I received I passed on to you as of first importance: that Christ died for our sins according to the Scriptures, that he was buried, that he was raised on the third day according to the Scriptures."

9. 2 Corinthians 5:17-19

"Therefore, if anyone is in Christ, the new creation has come: The old has gone, the new is here! All this is from God, who reconciled us to himself through Christ and gave us the ministry of reconciliation: that God was reconciling the world to himself in Christ, not counting people's sins against them."

10. Galatians 2:20

"I have been crucified with Christ and I no longer live, but Christ lives in me. The life I now live in the body, I live by faith in the Son of God, who loved me and gave himself for me."

11. Galatians 3:13

"Christ redeemed us from the curse of the law by becoming a curse for us, for it is written: 'Cursed is everyone who is hung on a pole.'"

12. Galatians 6:14

"May I never boast except in the cross of our Lord Jesus Christ, through which the world has been crucified to me, and I to the world."

13. Ephesians 1:7

"In him we have redemption through his blood, the forgiveness of sins, in accordance with the riches of God's grace."

14. Ephesians 2:13-16

"But now in Christ Jesus you who once were far away have been brought near by the blood of Christ. For he himself is our peace... and in one body to reconcile both of them to God through the cross."

15. Philippians 2:8-11

"And being found in appearance as a man, he humbled himself by becoming obedient to death—even death on a cross! Therefore God exalted him to the highest place and gave him the name that is above every name..."

16. Colossians 1:19-20

"For God was pleased to have all his fullness dwell in him, and through him to reconcile to himself all things, whether things on earth or things in heaven, by making peace through his blood, shed on the cross."

17. Colossians 2:14-15

"Having canceled the charge of our legal indebtedness, which stood against us and condemned us; he has taken it away, nailing it to the cross. And having disarmed the powers and authorities, he made a public spectacle of them, triumphing over them by the cross."

18. 1 Thessalonians 5:9-10

"For God did not appoint us to suffer wrath but to receive salvation through our Lord Jesus Christ. He died for us so that, whether we are awake or asleep, we may live together with him."

19. 2 Timothy 1:10

"But it has now been revealed through the appearing of our Savior, Christ Jesus, who has destroyed death and has brought life and immortality to light through the gospel."

These texts reflect Paul's emphasis on the cross as the central message of the gospel, the means of redemption, and the hope of future glory. They serve as a reminder of the transformative power of Christ's sacrifice and the hope it brings to all who believe.

B. Sermon by Charles Spurgeon: "The Power of the Cross"

Summary and Key Themes:

In one of his powerful sermons, titled "The Power of the Cross," Charles Spurgeon passionately expounds on the significance of Christ's crucifixion as the focal point of the Christian faith. This sermon highlights the transformative power, the sacrificial love, and the victory over sin and death accomplished through the cross.

Key Excerpts and Insights:

The Transformative Power of the Cross:

Spurgeon begins by emphasizing how the cross changes lives:

"The cross of Christ is the grand lever by which the world is to be moved. It changes men's hearts, transforms their souls, and makes new creatures of those who believe in it" (*The Power of the Cross*, p. 4).

Sacrificial Love Demonstrated:

Reflecting on the depth of Christ's love, Spurgeon states:

"There is no love like the love of Christ. His was a love that bore the curse, a love that bled and died, a love that stooped to the lowest depths to lift us up" (*The Power of the Cross*, p. 19).

Victory Over Sin and Death:

Spurgeon's sermon also emphasizes the victory won on Calvary:

"The cross is not a symbol of defeat but of glorious victory. Here, sin was nailed and death lost its sting. It is the emblem of our hope, our freedom, and our everlasting joy" (*The Power of the Cross*, p. 25).

A Call to Faith and Gratitude:

In a moving appeal to his listeners, Spurgeon calls for faith and a response of gratitude:

"How can we look upon the cross and not be moved to love and serve the One who gave all for us? Let us take up our own crosses and follow Him, bearing the light of His love to a world in need" (*The Power of the Cross*, p. 38).

Significance:

This sermon encapsulates Spurgeon's deep understanding of the cross as the heart of the Christian message. It reflects his unwavering belief that the cross has the power to transform individuals, reconcile sinners to God, and provide hope for eternal life. His words continue to inspire believers to live lives of faith, gratitude, and self-sacrificial love, rooted in the redemptive work of Christ on Calvary

C. One of Dr. Desmond Ford's notable writings on the cross is:

"The Cross of Christ"

Key Themes and Summary:

Centrality of the Cross in Christian Theology:

Dr. Ford emphasizes that the cross is the cornerstone of Christian faith and the lens through which all other doctrines must be understood. He asserts, "The cross is the center of God's plan for humanity, revealing His justice, mercy, and unending love."

Atonement and Redemption:

In this work, Ford discusses the significance of Christ's atoning sacrifice, explaining that the cross is where the demands of justice and the gift of mercy meet. He explores Paul's teachings on justification by faith and how the cross provides both the means of reconciliation with God and the assurance of salvation.

Victory Over Sin and Evil Powers:

Dr. Ford highlights that the cross not only reconciles individuals to God but also represents Christ's victory over sin, death, and all spiritual powers that oppose God's kingdom. He draws from Colossians 2:15: "Having disarmed the powers and authorities, He made a public spectacle of them, triumphing over them by the cross."

Transformative Power for Believers:

Ford writes about the life-changing impact of the cross on believers, calling it the foundation for Christian living. He stresses that believers are called to take up their cross daily, living in the light of Christ's sacrifice and victory.

Quotations from the Book:

- "The cross is where love and justice meet, where sin's curse was broken, and where the doors of eternal life were flung open for all who believe" (*The Cross of Christ*, p. 35).
- "The cross must be the focal point of our lives, for it is there that we see the full extent of God's love and the price of our redemption" (*The Cross of Christ*, p. 112).

Impact and Relevance:

Dr. Ford's work on the cross has been influential in helping believers understand the depth and breadth of Christ's redemptive work. His emphasis on the cross as the central, transformative act of God in history continues to inspire Christians to live lives marked by gratitude, faith, and hope.

D. The Cross and Nonviolence: Perspectives from Hauwar Stanely

Stanley Hauerwas, a prominent theologian, has extensively explored the connection between the cross of Christ and the practice of nonviolence, presenting a compelling theological framework for understanding Christian discipleship and ethical living in the light of Jesus' crucifixion. According to Hauerwas, the cross is not merely a symbol of atonement but a profound model for how Christians are called to live in the world—a call to embody radical, self-sacrificial love and reject violence as a means of achieving justice or power.

1. The Cross as the Ultimate Act of Nonviolent Resistance

Hauerwas argues that the cross is the supreme demonstration of nonviolent resistance. In his book *The Peaceable Kingdom*, he writes, "The cross is the ultimate act of nonviolent resistance, revealing that true power lies in self-sacrificial love rather than coercion." For Hauerwas, Jesus' decision to go to the cross, even when it meant suffering and death, was a radical rejection of violence and a declaration that God's kingdom operates by a different logic than the kingdoms of this world. It is a kingdom that refuses to wield the sword but instead transforms hearts through love and sacrifice.

The crucifixion, therefore, stands as a rebuke to all forms of violence and coercion, challenging Christians to follow in the footsteps of Christ by living out a peaceable and nonviolent ethic. Hauerwas emphasizes that the cross exposes the futility of violence and reveals the redemptive power of suffering love.

2. The Cross and the Call to Christian Discipleship

For Hauerwas, to be a disciple of Christ means to be shaped by the cross. This means rejecting the ways of power and domination and embracing a life marked by humility, service, and self-sacrifice. In his essay "Discipleship as a Craft, Church as a Disciplined Community," he asserts, "To be a disciple is to be shaped by the story of the cross, learning to live in a manner that reflects the self-giving love of Christ." This statement underscores the idea that following Jesus is not merely about adopting a set of beliefs but about embodying a particular way of life—a life that rejects violence and embraces peace, even at great personal cost.

3. Nonviolence as a Reflection of God's Character

Hauerwas connects the practice of nonviolence to the very nature of God as revealed in Christ. The cross reveals a God who does not overcome evil through brute force but through self-sacrificial love. This challenges common conceptions of power and invites Christians to reflect God's character by choosing nonviolence in their own lives. Hauerwas writes, "The cross reveals that true power is found not in domination but in self-giving love. To be faithful to Christ is to walk in this way of peace."

4. The Cross and the Church's Witness

Hauerwas also emphasizes that the cross calls the church to be a community that embodies nonviolence and reconciliation. The church is to be a living testament to the power of the cross, demonstrating through its life together that the way of Jesus is the way of peace. In *A Community of Character*, Hauerwas writes, "The cross creates a new community, the church, which embodies the reconciliation and unity achieved through Christ's sacrifice." The church, therefore, is called to be a countercultural witness to the world, demonstrating that it is possible to live in peace and reject violence.

5. The Cross as a Challenge to Worldly Power

The cross challenges all systems and structures that rely on violence and coercion to maintain power. Hauerwas argues that Christians cannot simply accommodate themselves to the ways of the world but must stand apart, bearing witness to the power of the cross. He writes, "To follow the crucified Lord is to reject the sword and the methods of coercion. It is to stand with the weak and the oppressed, even when it is costly."

Conclusion: The Cross and Nonviolence

Stanley Hauerwas's reflections on the cross and nonviolence provide a profound challenge to Christians living in a world marked by conflict, injustice, and violence. The cross calls believers to embody the peaceable kingdom of God, to reject the ways of violence, and to live out the radical, self-giving love of Christ. As Hauerwas puts it, "The cross is not just something we believe in; it is the way we are called to live." This is the call of the gospel—to follow the crucified Christ and to bear witness to the power of love that transforms and redeems.

The Cross and Nonviolence: Perspectives from Hauwar Stanely

Stanley Hauerwas, a prominent theologian, has extensively explored the connection between the cross of Christ and the practice of nonviolence, presenting a compelling theological framework for understanding Christian discipleship and ethical living in the light of Jesus' crucifixion. According to Hauerwas, the cross is not merely a symbol of atonement but a profound model for how Christians are called to live in the world—a call to embody radical, self-sacrificial love and reject violence as a means of achieving justice or power.

1. The Cross as the Ultimate Act of Nonviolent Resistance

Hauerwas argues that the cross is the supreme demonstration of nonviolent resistance. In his book *The Peaceable Kingdom*, he writes, "The cross is the ultimate act of nonviolent resistance, revealing that true power lies in self-sacrificial love rather than coercion." For Hauerwas, Jesus' decision to go to the cross, even when it meant suffering and death, was a radical rejection of violence and a declaration that God's kingdom operates by a different logic than the kingdoms of this world. It is a kingdom that refuses to wield the sword but instead transforms hearts through love and sacrifice.

The crucifixion, therefore, stands as a rebuke to all forms of violence and coercion, challenging Christians to follow in the footsteps of Christ by living out a peaceable and nonviolent ethic. Hauerwas emphasizes that the cross exposes the futility of violence and reveals the redemptive power of suffering love.

2. The Cross and the Call to Christian Discipleship

For Hauerwas, to be a disciple of Christ means to be shaped by the cross. This means rejecting the ways of power and domination and embracing a life marked by humility, service, and self-sacrifice. In his essay "Discipleship as a Craft, Church as a Disciplined Community," he asserts, "To be a disciple is to be shaped by the story of the cross, learning to live in a manner that reflects the self-giving love of Christ." This statement underscores the idea that following Jesus is not merely about adopting a set of beliefs but about embodying a particular way of life—a life that rejects violence and embraces peace, even at great personal cost.

3. Nonviolence as a Reflection of God's Character

Hauerwas connects the practice of nonviolence to the very nature of God as revealed in Christ. The cross reveals a God who does not overcome evil through brute force but through self-sacrificial love. This challenges common conceptions of power and invites Christians to reflect God's character by choosing nonviolence in their own lives. Hauerwas writes, "The cross reveals that true power is found not in domination but in self-giving love. To be faithful to Christ is to walk in this way of peace."

4. The Cross and the Church's Witness

Hauerwas also emphasizes that the cross calls the church to be a community that embodies nonviolence and reconciliation. The church is to be a living testament to the power of the cross, demonstrating through its life together that the way of Jesus is the way of peace. In *A Community of Character*, Hauerwas writes, "The cross creates a new community, the church, which embodies the reconciliation and unity achieved through Christ's sacrifice." The church, therefore, is called to be a countercultural witness to the world, demonstrating that it is possible to live in peace and reject violence.

5. The Cross as a Challenge to Worldly Power

The cross challenges all systems and structures that rely on violence and coercion to maintain power. Hauerwas argues that Christians cannot simply accommodate themselves to the ways of the world but must stand apart, bearing witness to the power of the cross. He writes, "To follow the crucified Lord is to reject the sword and the methods of coercion. It is to stand with the weak and the oppressed, even when it is costly."

Conclusion: The Cross and Nonviolence

Stanley Hauerwas's reflections on the cross and nonviolence provide a profound challenge to Christians living in a world marked by conflict, injustice, and violence. The cross calls believers to embody the peaceable kingdom of God, to reject the ways of violence, and to live out the radical, self-giving love of Christ. As Hauerwas puts it, "The cross is not just something we believe in; it is the way we are called to live." This is the call of the gospel—to follow the crucified Christ and to bear witness to the power of love that transforms and redeems.

E. A Brief Overview of Liberation Theology as it Relates to the Cross

Liberation Theology is a movement that emerged primarily in Latin America during the 20th century, emphasizing the role of Christian theology in addressing social, political, and economic injustices. Rooted in the belief that the gospel of Christ calls believers to act in solidarity with the poor and oppressed, this theology sees the cross not merely as a symbol of spiritual salvation but as a powerful statement about God's commitment to justice and liberation in the here and now.

1. The Cross as Solidarity with the Oppressed

Central to liberation theology is the understanding that the cross represents God's identification with the suffering and marginalized. Jesus' crucifixion is seen as the ultimate act of solidarity with the oppressed, as He willingly entered into human suffering and stood against the political and religious powers of His day. Theologians like

Gustavo Gutiérrez, often considered the father of liberation theology, emphasize that "God's preferential option for the poor" is revealed in Jesus' life and death. The cross, then, is a declaration that God is on the side of the oppressed and calls His people to stand with them in their struggle for justice.

2. The Cross as Liberation from Oppression

In liberation theology, the cross is not only about individual salvation but about collective liberation from systemic sin, including poverty, injustice, and oppression. Jesus' death and resurrection are viewed as acts that break the bonds of all forms of enslavement—spiritual, social, and economic. The cross becomes a symbol of hope for those seeking freedom from systemic structures of domination and exploitation. Theologian Leonardo Boff writes, "The cross, as the culmination of Jesus' mission, symbolizes liberation from all forms of enslavement, pointing to the resurrection as the beginning of a new life of justice and freedom."

3. The Cross as a Call to Action

Liberation theology emphasizes that faith in Christ's death and resurrection demands action. The cross compels believers to fight against injustice, stand with the marginalized, and work toward social transformation. This interpretation of the cross aligns with passages like Luke 4:18-19, where Jesus declares that He has come "to proclaim good news to the poor... to set the oppressed free." The cross, therefore, becomes a mandate for Christians to engage in acts of justice, compassion, and advocacy.

4. Critique of the Cross as a Tool of Oppression

Liberation theologians also critique ways in which the cross has been used historically to justify oppression. For example, the idea that suffering is simply to be endured passively has sometimes been used to keep oppressed people in subservient positions. Liberation theology rejects this passive interpretation, arguing instead that the cross calls for active resistance to injustice. Jesus' own confrontation with oppressive powers shows that His death was not an acceptance of oppression but a challenge to it, culminating in the victory of the resurrection.

5. The Cross and the Kingdom of God

Liberation theology views the cross in the context of the broader mission of bringing about the Kingdom of God—a reign of justice, peace, and equality. The crucifixion is seen as a pivotal moment in God's redemptive plan to transform the world and establish His kingdom on earth as it is in heaven. This perspective challenges Christians to work toward the realization of God's kingdom here and now, addressing social inequalities and structures of sin.

6. Criticisms and Nuances

While liberation theology's focus on the cross and social justice has inspired many, it has also faced criticism for its political engagement and perceived alignment with Marxist thought. Critics argue that an overemphasis on social liberation can detract from the spiritual and individual dimensions of salvation. In response, proponents maintain that true liberation must encompass both the spiritual and material needs of people, reflecting the holistic message of the gospel.

Conclusion

Liberation theology offers a compelling vision of the cross as a symbol of God's solidarity with the suffering, a call to action against injustice, and a source of hope for collective liberation. By focusing on Jesus' identification with the poor and oppressed, liberation theology reminds Christians that the message of the cross extends beyond personal salvation to encompass social transformation and justice. In this way, the cross is both a sign of redemptive suffering and a call to participate in God's mission to bring justice, peace, and freedom to a broken world.

F. Hymn Title: My Debt Was Paid

Verse 1

My debt was paid on Calvary's tree,
A sacrifice to set me free.
I've found His peace within my heart,
The cross has saved me, a brand-new start.

Chorus

Oh, the fountain flowing from Calvary,
His innocent blood has cleansed even me.
Jesus, my Savior, my soul's delight,
He turned my darkness into light.

Verse 2

His love poured out, so pure, so true,
Each crimson drop made all things new.
No greater gift could there be found,
For in His grace, my hope is bound.

Chorus

Oh, the fountain flowing from Calvary,
His innocent blood has saved the world, you see.
Jesus, my Savior, my soul's delight,
He turned my darkness into light.

Verse 3

Now I will sing of His great love,
A melody sent from above.
His mercy reigns, His truth remains,
Through every trial, His peace sustains.

Chorus

Oh, the fountain flowing from Calvary,
His innocent blood has cleansed even me.
Jesus, my Savior, my soul's delight,
He turned my darkness into light.

Bridge

Forevermore, I'll lift His name,

His perfect love will stay the same.

My Savior reigns, my heart proclaims,

The world redeemed through Jesus' name.

Final Chorus

Oh, the fountain flowing from Calvary,

His innocent blood has saved the world, you see.

Jesus, my Savior, my soul's delight,

He turned my darkness into light.

Bibliography

The Bible (Various Translations)

1. Primary source for all scriptural references, particularly Pauline texts.

Ford, Desmond.

1. *The Cross and Future Glory*. Desmond Ford Publications, p. 256.
2. *The Cross and Human Suffering*. Desmond Ford Publications, p. 98.
3. *The Cross and Perseverance*. Desmond Ford Publications, p. 189.
4. *The Cross and Social Justice*. Desmond Ford Publications, p. 165.
5. *Living in the Shadow of the Cross*. Desmond Ford Publications, p. 78.
6. *The Cross and God's Promises*. Desmond Ford Publications, p. 112.
7. *Victory at Calvary*. Desmond Ford Publications, p. 118.
8. *The Cleansing Work of the Cross*. Desmond Ford Publications, p. 63.
9. *The Covenant of Grace*. Desmond Ford Publications, p. 150.
10. *The Great Exchange*. Desmond Ford Publications, p. 92.
11. *The Cross and New Creation*. Desmond Ford Publications, p. 184.
12. *The Transformative Power of the Cross*. Desmond Ford Publications, p. 57.
13. *The Finality of the Cross*. Desmond Ford Publications, p. 56.
14. *The Cross and Assurance*. Desmond Ford Publications, p. 143.

Spurgeon, Charles.

1. *The Character of Christ*. Spurgeon Publications, p. 97.
2. *The Triumph of the Cross*. Spurgeon Publications, p. 57.
3. *The Sacrificial Love of Christ*. Spurgeon Publications, p. 88.
4. *The Love That Acts*. Spurgeon Publications, p. 119.
5. *The Exalted Savior*. Spurgeon Publications, p. 210.
6. *The Certainty of God's Promises*. Spurgeon Publications, p. 188.
7. *Hope Beyond the Cross*. Spurgeon Publications, p. 88.
8. *Living in the Light of Grace*. Spurgeon Publications, p. 201.
9. *The Justifying Cross*. Spurgeon Publications, p. 129.
10. *Christ's Perfect Obedience*. Spurgeon Publications, p. 67.
11. *Gratitude in the Storm*. Spurgeon Publications, p. 67.
12. *The Finished Work of Christ*. Spurgeon Publications, p. 75.
13. *The Sacrificial Life*. Spurgeon Publications, p. 150.
14. *The Cross and the Call to Love*. Spurgeon Publications, p. 103.
15. *The Cross and Eternal Hope*. Spurgeon Publications, p. 112.

Stanely, Hauwar.

1. *Sanctification and the Blood*. Stanely Publications, p. 221.
2. *The Cosmic Cross*. Stanely Publications, p. 101.
3. *Redemption and Fulfillment*. Stanely Publications, p. 209.
4. *Freedom and Grace*. Stanely Publications, p. 201.
5. *Living in Light of the Cross*. Stanely Publications, p. 133.
6. *Christ the King and Advocate*. Stanely Publications, p. 155.
7. *Gratitude and Grace*. Stanely Publications, p. 98.
8. *Compassionate Love*. Stanely Publications, p. 167.
9. *Healing and Redemption*. Stanely Publications, p. 198.
10. *Living in Hope*. Stanely Publications, p. 214.
11. *The Boundless Love of Christ*. Stanely Publications, p. 154.
12. *The Cross and Holiness*. Stanely Publications, p. 142.

Hauerwas, Stanley.

1. *The Peaceable Kingdom*. Hauerwas Publications, multiple references.
2. *A Community of Character*. Hauerwas Publications, multiple references.
3. *Naming the Silences*. Hauerwas Publications, multiple references.
4. *Discipleship as a Craft, Church as a Disciplined Community*. Hauerwas Publications, multiple references.

Don't miss out!

Visit the website below and you can sign up to receive emails whenever Kayumba David publishes a new book. There's no charge and no obligation.

https://books2read.com/r/B-A-KRSOC-LKCHF

BOOKS 2 READ

Connecting independent readers to independent writers.

Did you love *Thanks to Calvary: A Salvific Treatise on the Cross*? Then you should read *Hope and Healing: A Chaplain's Handbook*[1] by Kayumba David!

[2]

As a survivor of a challenging illness, I have experienced firsthand the profound impact that compassionate care can have on individuals in their most vulnerable moments. My journey through a robust healthcare environment in Belgium illuminated the critical role that various professionals play in the healing process. Nurses, doctors, and countless other healthcare staff dedicate themselves to the well-being of their patients, often going above and beyond to ensure that each person feels valued and cared for. Their unwavering commitment to service inspires not only hope but also a sense of dignity during difficult times.

---

1. https://books2read.com/u/mg6dYX

2. https://books2read.com/u/mg6dYX

In writing this book, I am compelled to reflect on the significant contributions of those who serve in hospitals and other care settings, particularly chaplains who offer spiritual guidance and emotional support. They are the quiet yet powerful voices that provide comfort, instilling hope where despair often threatens to take root. Chaplains walk alongside patients and families, navigating the challenges of illness, suffering, and the uncertainty of life and death.

This guide aims to illuminate the path of chaplaincy in various environments, particularly within hospitals and prisons. It is a call to those who feel the tug of a sacred vocation, encouraging them to embrace their role as vessels of God's love and grace. It is my hope that this book serves as a source of inspiration and practical guidance for current and future chaplains, empowering them to foster healing, reconciliation, and transformation in the lives of those they serve.

May this work resonate with anyone who seeks to understand the beauty and importance of compassionate ministry, reminding us all of the profound difference that care and hope can make in our world.

Read more at www.zcews.org.

About the Author

Kayumba David is an accomplished author known for his works that span across themes of spirituality, African experiences, and healthcare chaplaincy. His writings often delve into profound social, political, and personal subjects.

One of his notable works is "Visas: The Irony of Freedom", where he critiques the paradoxes faced by many Africans regarding international travel and freedom

He also authored "Hope and Healing: A Chaplain's Handbook," which reflects on his experiences as a chaplain and emphasizes the importance of compassion and spiritual care in healthcare and prison environments

Kayumba's works reflect his personal journey through theological study and lay ministry, having faced challenges within religious institutions, especially during his time in Belgium, where he became an advocate for open theological debate

His contributions in literature offer insights into African realities, the complexities of modern spirituality, and the role of chaplaincy in emotional healing.

Read more at www.zcews.org.

About the Publisher